UNEP YEAR BOOK

EMERGING ISSUES
IN OUR GLOBAL ENVIRONMENT

2014

UNEP

United Nations Environment Programme

Table of Contents

Foreword

Ten years ago UNEP alerted the world to the development of dead zones in coastal waters resulting from excess nitrogen seeping into the water. That was in the first edition of the Year Book series. In the intervening period many more emerging issues have been identified, with some rising to crisis level and others showing encouraging improvement.

The 2014 Year Book shows how scientific endeavour and policy actions have led to innovative solutions and vital advancements. Yet these are frequently outpaced by overall economic growth. For example, as the fuel efficiency of cars has increased, the size of the vehicle fleet continues to grow. Similarly, as the aquaculture sector expands in response to the demand for food, scientists expect that its environmental impacts may double by 2030. For the illegal wildlife trade, a state of crisis has been reached, with the world standing to lose two iconic species as a result of the demand for ivory and rhino horn if no urgent action is taken.

The 2014 Year Book reconfirms the critical role that the environment plays in maintaining and improving the health of people and ecosystems: from the well-managed soils and nutrients that underpin food production to the critical role of biodiversity in protecting human health against the spread of infectious diseases. Clean air in our cities prevents the premature death and illness of millions of people and can save society trillions of dollars.

Our economies are still largely fossil-fuel based, with the environmental, economic and health costs largely hidden. For example, in the pristine polar regions, scientists have recently found tiny pieces of plastic trapped in sea ice. Transported by ocean currents across great distances, these contaminated particles eventually can become a source of chemicals in our food. The key of course is to prevent plastic debris from entering the environment in the first place.

The issues in the 2014 Year Book have clear connections. A warmer and wetter climate will cause shifts in the spread of infectious diseases, whilst rapid melting of Arctic glaciers will have far-reaching global implications for sea-level rise and the potential release of methane – a potent greenhouse gas. Strong action on air pollutants, especially particulate matter – of which black carbon is a component – would result in multiple benefits by not only slowing the melting of polar ice and snow, but also significantly improving human health.

A key message of the 2014 Year Book is that we will increasingly need access to timely, reliable environmental information from locations around the world so that we can identify issues as they emerge and develop effective actions and policies to respond to them. Without this, the global community's efforts will be hampered. It is for this reason that UNEP is committed to helping countries improve their environmental data flow and to making knowledge much more widely accessible. From new space technologies to social media and citizen science, UNEP is supporting local and indigenous communities to start measuring and providing data themselves. The Year Book itself reflects this change by being launched as a mobile app, richly illustrating the topics with live graphics and video stories about positive initiatives that address existing and emerging issues.

I encourage you to explore the Year Book in its new format and use the 2014 Year Book update to support your own activities in the advancement of sustainable development.

Achim Steiner

United Nations Under-Secretary-General and Executive Director,
United Nations Environment Programme

UNEP Year Book 2014 emerging issues update

Excess Nitrogen in the Environment

Changes in the global nitrogen cycle

Nitrogen is an essential nutrient for plant growth. The discovery a century ago of an industrial process that converted nitrogen in the air to ammonia made the *manufacture of nitrogen fertilizers* possible. This discovery was followed by a spectacular increase in global food production.

Nitrogen fertilizers: 100 years of using the Haber-Bosch process

There is an abundance of nitrogen in the atmosphere, but this nitrogen exists almost entirely in a form that is unusable by most organisms. Atmospheric nitrogen can be made usable or 'reactive' through natural processes (e.g. nitrogen fixation by legumes such as soybeans) or artificially. The Haber-Bosch process is essential for the manufacture of fertilizers containing nitrogen, which were first produced on an industrial scale in 1913.

Today nitrogen and other nutrients are used inefficiently in most of the world's agricultural systems – resulting in enormous and largely unnecessary losses to the environment, with profound impacts ranging from air and water pollution to the undermining of important ecosystems (and the services and livelihoods they support). Such impacts are often more visible in developed regions than in developing ones.

The global nitrogen cycle has been profoundly altered by human activity over the past century. The amount of usable or 'reactive' nitrogen produced by humans (about 190 million tonnes per year) is now greater than the amount created through natural processes (112 million tonnes per year). In addition to inefficient application of nitrogen fertilizers, sources of excess nitrogen in the environment are inadequately treated animal and human wastes and fossil fuel combustion in transport and in energy production, which creates nitrogen oxides.

As nitrogen moves through the environment, the same nitrogen atom can contribute to multiple negative effects in the air, on land, in freshwater and marine systems, and on human health. This sequence continues over a long period and is referred to as the 'nitrogen cascade'.

Nitrogen does not move through all environmental systems at the same rate. For example, soil, forests and grasslands accumulate it, which can lead to slowing of the nitrogen cascade, while air transfers the nitrogen more rapidly. Excess nitrogen in the environment contributes to many health and environmental problems, including:

- Coastal dead zones and fish kills due to severe eutrophication or hypoxia resulting from nitrate run-off and leaching into river systems
- Biodiversity loss in terrestrial, freshwater and coastal water systems due to eutrophication and acidification
- Groundwater pollution by nitrates
- Freshwater pollution due to eutrophication and acidification
- Human health impacts resulting from the formation of aerosols and ground-level (tropospheric) ozone, a main component of smog, causing respiratory diseases
- Reduced crop, forest and grassland productivity due to nitrogen deposition and over-fertilization, as well as ground-level ozone exposure
- Global climate change and the depletion of stratospheric ozone, which protects life on Earth from harmful ultraviolet (UV) rays

Read more about the nitrogen cascade in the 2003 Year Book.

Simplified view of the nitrogen cascade

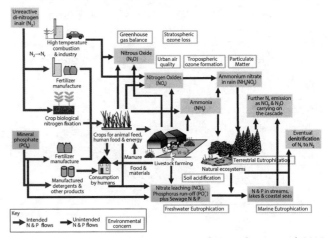

Source: Sutton et al. 2013

Increased coastal dead zones and climate change impacts

Ongoing research is improving our understanding of how excess nitrogen affects air, water and soil quality, puts pressure on ecosystems and biodiversity, leads to human health risks, and affects the global climate. Because of human modification of the nitrogen cycle, thresholds for reactive nitrogen have already been exceeded in some places – with the risk of bringing about abrupt or irreversible environmental changes.

Organisms require oxygen to grow and reproduce. 'Dead zones' are oxygen-depleted (hypoxic) areas that result from over-enrichment of waters with nutrients (especially nitrogen and phosphorus), for example from fertilizer run-off, industrial waste and sewage. Reported cases of coastal dead zones have doubled in each of the last four decades. There are currently over 500 known dead zones in the world, whereas in 2003 only around 150 such oxygen-depleted areas were reported. Close to 1000 other coastal and marine areas are experiencing the effects of eutrophication. The number of areas identified as suffering from hypoxia is increasing most rapidly in the developing world. Rapid increases in algae growth in aquatic systems (algal blooms) are stimulated by nutrient enrichment. They can include toxic algae or algae that, after deposition, cause damage to living coral reefs.

Nitrogen emissions to the air – notably those of *nitrous oxide* (N_2O) – are contributing to climate change. Nitrous oxide is naturally present in relatively small quantities in the atmosphere as part of the nitrogen cycle. However, human activities such as agriculture and deforestation, fossil fuel combustion, industrial processes and wastewater management are increasing the amount in the atmosphere.

Nitrous oxide: the 'forgotten greenhouse gas'

Nitrous oxide (N_2O) emissions continue to increase globally. N_2O is a powerful greenhouse gas that causes stratospheric ozone layer depletion. Sometimes referred to as the 'forgotten greenhouse gas', it is over 300 times more effective at trapping heat in the atmosphere than carbon dioxide (CO_2) over a 100-year period.

More than two-thirds of atmospheric emissions of nitrous oxide arise from processes in soils, largely resulting from application of nitrogen fertilizers. Some countries are experiencing intense air pollution, much of which is due to nitrogen emissions. These emissions result in deposition of nitrogen in terrestrial and aquatic ecosystems, with implications for human and ecosystem health, biodiversity and climate change. Nitrogen deposition rates in the industrialized and agriculturally intensified regions of China are reportedly as high as the peak rates in northwestern Europe in the 1980s, before the introduction of nitrogen emission mitigation measures.

Nitrogen plays a critical role in climate change mitigation, adaptation and impacts. It has been suggested that nitrogen has a net cooling effect on climate change through the contribution of aerosols (suspensions of tiny particles formed from nitrous oxide, nitrogen oxide and ammonia that scatter sunlight) and biomass growth in terrestrial and aquatic systems due to nitrogen fertilization, which leads to greater carbon dioxide (CO_2) uptake. Climate warming results from increased nitrous oxide emissions, ground-level ozone production, and damage to vegetation because of over-fertilization with nitrogen. Even with the net cooling effect, therefore, much can be done to reduce nitrogen's warming impacts and contribute to efforts to tackle climate change.

© http://www.daypic.ru

What is being done to reduce excess nitrogen releases?

In 2011 governments agreed to address the nitrogen challenge by endorsing the Global Partnership of Nutrient Management (GPNM). Established in 2009, GPNM is a multi-stakeholder partnership made up of governments, the private sector, the scientific community, civil society organizations and UN agencies – all committed to promoting effective nutrient management in order to achieve food security (through increased productivity), conservation of natural resources and environmental protection. By means of GPNM, countries and other stakeholders identify opportunities for co-operative work across international and regional fora and agencies addressing nutrients.

In the 2012 UN Conference on Sustainable Development (Rio+20) outcome document 'The Future We Want', governments also 'noted with concern that the health of oceans and marine biodiversity are negatively affected by (…) nitrogen-based compounds, from a number of marine and land-based sources.' World leaders at Rio+20 made a commitment to act to reduce the incidence and impacts of such pollution on marine ecosystems. This commitment by the global community needs to be taken forward through a concerted programme of actions, including creating greater awareness of the urgent need for better nutrient management and waste treatment.

A number of tools have been developed in recent years to increase awareness of the nitrogen issue by decision makers and the general public, as well as to educate farmers and others in the agricultural sector on better nutrient management. These include the N-Calculator, a 'nitrogen footprint' model, N-Sink, a simple geo-spatial tool designed for watershed managers, and N-Visualisation, a tool with animations that helps users understand the effects of different measures on the environment, economies and land use.

Fertilizer best management practices are designed to maximize the benefits of using manufactured fertilizers worldwide and to minimize the negative impacts of their misuse or over-use. There is considerable scope for farmers using fertilizers to improve the efficiency of their nutrient management. For example, despite the 1991 European Union (EU) Nitrates Directive, which is intended to prevent nitrates from agricultural sources polluting ground and surface waters, only two EU countries, Denmark and the Netherlands, have reduced this type of nitrogen pollution so far.

One reason for inefficient nutrient use is the existence of fertilizer subsidies in many countries. Furthermore, education and extension services often focus on increasing production through fertilizer use, rather than on applying fertilizer more efficiently in view of the negative environmental impacts of excessive nitrogen inputs.

Better management practices are essential to improve nitrogen use efficiency. This is the most cost-effective option for reducing nitrogen losses to the environment from agricultural sources. There are large variations in farm types and sizes, climatic conditions, soils and other factors. Adequate and appropriate guidelines, educational programmes and independent extension services are required throughout the world.

Technological innovations can also limit the amount of nitrogen released to the environment, while ensuring food security for billions of people. Controlled-release fertilizers and fertilizer deep placement are examples. Such innovations are aimed at increasing crop yields and farmers' incomes while reducing the amount of fertilizer used and lessening environmental damage.

The volume of sewage and industrial waste generated by a growing world population has increased nitrogen inputs to the environment. In developing countries, fewer than 35% of cities have any form of sewage treatment. Where such facilities exist, they often provide only primary treatment, which does little to remove nitrogen. Even in the developed world, many sewage treatment facilities do not include the tertiary treatment that removes most of the nitrogen.

There is wide recognition that the nitrogen issue needs to be better understood and communicated in order to reduce losses to the environment and create the momentum to take effective action. In particular, awareness is needed of the environmental and human health consequences of ever-increasing nitrogen inputs, including nitrogen's critical role in climate change mitigation, adaptation and impacts.

Towards integrated nitrogen management

Our knowledge of the nitrogen cycle has improved in the last decade, along with our ability to quantify the sources, fate and impacts of nitrogen in the environment. However, because of the complexity of the nitrogen cycle and the different scales involved (from local to global), scientific understanding and measures to reduce nitrogen pollution are often focused on individual sectors.

There is also a fragmentation of the policies that address aspects of the nitrogen challenge. These policies typically focus on environmental compartments (e.g. air, water, soil), particular environmental issues (e.g. waste management, biodiversity loss, climate change) or a single form of nitrogen (e.g. nitrates, nitrogen oxides).

The scale on which stakeholders operate also differs, ranging from the global commodity level in the case of the fertilizer industry to small-scale farmers and local communities. More comprehensive, integrated management is needed to reduce the adverse effects of excess nitrogen in the environment while optimizing food production and energy use. There is an urgent need to:

- Develop joined-up approaches that take into account impacts on the nitrogen cycle in, for example, the production and consumption of food and energy, as well as the risks to ecosystems, biodiversity, the climate and human health
- Establish internationally agreed targets for integrated nitrogen management
- Coordinate (and collaborate) among regions and locations in order to make the large improvements needed in global nitrogen use efficiency

One of the key messages of the recent 'Our Nutrient World' report is that a 20% improvement in global nutrient use efficiency by 2020 would reduce annual use of nitrogen fertilizer by an estimated 20 million tonnes. This, in turn, could produce net savings of US$50-400 billion per year in terms of improvements in human health, climate and biodiversity.

Society faces profound challenges in trying to meet global demands for food, fibre and fuel while minimizing nitrogen's unintended negative environmental and human health impacts. Effective management policies need to be in place to prevent or reduce air pollution, eutrophication and climate effects, among others. A number of key actions for more effective management have been proposed that could reduce the amount of nitrogen entering the environment, using an integrated approach. Generally these include the following:

- Focusing on natural production (nitrogen 'fixing') while limiting flows of reactive nitrogen
- Fixing nitrogen in such a way that it does not find its way back into the environment, and, if possible, reuse nitrogen
- Using technology that converts nitrogen back into unreactive nitrogen (N_2) as soon as possible

Technological innovations – and wide dissemination of these technologies and of good practices – are crucial. However, the immense impacts of human activities on the nitrogen cycle, especially since the mid 20th century, also call for re-evaluating 21st century consumption patterns – that is, our nitrogen footprint.

Source: Sutton et al. 2013

Further information about excess nitrogen in the environment

Davidson, E.A., et al. (2012). Excess nitrogen in the U.S. environment: Trends, risks, and solutions. Issues in Ecology Report No. 15. Ecological Society of America http://www.whrc.org/resources/publications/pdf/DavidsonetalIssuesEcol.12.pdf

Díaz, R., et al. (2012). Agriculture's Impact on Aquaculture: Hypoxia and Eutrophication in Marine Waters. OECD http://www.oecd.org/tad/sustainable-agriculture/49841630.pdf

EC (2013). Science for Environment Policy. Nitrogen Pollution and the European Environment Implications for Air Quality Policy http://www.ec.europa.eu/environment/integration/research/newsalert/pdf/IR6.pdf

Erisman, J.W. et al. (2013). Consequences of human modification of the global nitrogen cycle. Phil. Trans. Roy. Soc. 368 (1621) http://www.rstb.royalsocietypublishing.org/content/368/1621/20130116.short

Erisman, J.W. et al. (2011). Reactive nitrogen in the environment and its effect on climate change, Current Opinion in Environmental Sustainability 3 (5), 281-290 http://www.researchgate.net/publication/230619445_Reactive_nitrogen_in_the_environment_and_its_effect_on_climate_change

Erisman, J.W. et al. (2008). How a century of ammonia synthesis changed the world. Nature Geoscience 1, 636 - 639 http://www.nature.com/ngeo/journal/v1/n10/abs/ngeo325.html

Fowler, D., et al. (2013). The global nitrogen cycle in the twenty-first century: introduction. Philosophical Transactions of the Royal Society. B: Biological Sciences, 368, 1621 http://www.rstb.royalsocietypublishing.org/content/368/1621/20130165.full

Galloway, J.N. et al. (2003). The nitrogen cascade. BioScience, 53 (4), 341-356.

Galloway, J., et al. (2008). Transformation of the nitrogen cycle: Recent trends, questions, and potential solutions. Science, 320 (5878), 889-892 http://www.sciencemag.org/content/320/5878/889

Leach, A.M. et al. (2012). A nitrogen footprint model to help consumers understand their role in nitrogen losses to the environment. Environmental Development 1, 40–66 http://www.sciencedirect.com/science/article/pii/S221146451100008X

Liu, X., et al. (2013). Enhanced nitrogen deposition over China. Nature, 494, 459-462 http://www.nature.com/nature/journal/v494/n7438/pdf/nature11917.pdf

Noone, K.J., et al. (2013). Managing Ocean Environments in a Changing Climate: Sustainability and Economic Perspectives. Elsevier http://www.sciencedirect.com/science/book/9780124076686

STAP (Scientific and Technical Advisory Panel) (2011). Hypoxia and Nutrient Reduction in the Coastal Zone. Advice for Prevention, Remediation and Research. A STAP Advisory Document. Global Environment Facility http://www.thegef.org/gef/sites/thegef.org/files/publication/STAP_Hypoxia_low.pdf

Suddick, E.C., et al. (2013). The role of nitrogen in climate change and the impacts of nitrogen-climate interactions in the United States: foreword to thematic issue. Biogeochemistry, 114:1-10 http://www.link.springer.com/article/10.1007/s10533-012-9795-z#page-1

Sutton, M. A., et al. (2011). The European Nitrogen Assessment: Sources, Effects and Policy Perspectives. Cambridge University Press; Summary for Policy Makers http://www.assets.cambridge.org/97811070/06126/frontmatter/9781107006126_frontmatter.pdf

Sutton, M.A., et al. (2013). Our Nutrient World. The challenge to produce more food and energy with less pollution http://www.gpa.unep.org/index.php/global-partnership-on-nutrient-management/publications-and-resources/global-partnership-on-nutrient-management-gpnm/143-our-nutrient-world

Thompson, A.J., et al. (eds.) (2012a). Meeting Issue "Nitrous oxide: the forgotten greenhouse gas". Philosophical Transactions of the Royal Society. B: Biological Sciences, 367 http://www.rstb.royalsocietypublishing.org/site/2012/nitrous_oxide.xhtml

UNDESA, UN-DOALOS/OLA, IAEA, IMO, IOC-UNESCO, UNDP, UNEP, UNWTO (2014). How oceans- and seas-related measures contribute to the economic, social and environmental dimensions of sustainable development: Local and regional experiences http://www.sustainabledevelopment.un.org/content/documents/1339Non_recurrent_e_publication_Oceans_final%20version.pdf

UNEP (2013). Drawing Down N2O to Protect Climate and the Ozone Layer. A UNEP Synthesis Report. United Nations Environment Programme (UNEP), Nairobi, Kenya http://www.unep.org/publications/ebooks/UNEPN2Oreport/

UNEP and Woods Hole Research Center (2007). Reactive Nitrogen in the Environment: Too Much or Too Little of a Good Thing http://www.unep.fr/scp/publications/details.asp?id=DTI/0904/PA

World Resources Institute (2013). Interactive Map of Eutrophication & Hypoxia http://www.wri.org/our-work/project/eutrophication-and-hypoxia

UNEP Year Book 2014 emerging issues update

The Emergence of Infectious Diseases

Emergence and re-emergence of infectious diseases

Severe acute respiratory syndrome (SARS) was first reported in Asia in February 2003. Before this viral respiratory illness was officially declared contained just five months later, it had spread to more than two dozen countries in North and South America, Europe and Asia, killing 774 people and making more than 8000 others ill. The SARS outbreak – caused by a previously unknown coronavirus (SARS-CoV) which likely had spread from bats to humans – was a stunning example of human populations, economic activities, environmental conditions and air travel coming together, creating a global health threat.

Human infectious diseases are caused by pathogenic microorganisms such as bacteria, viruses, parasites and fungi that spread directly or indirectly via a *vector* from one person to another or from an animal to people. The 2004/5 Year Book reported that 15 million people died annually from infectious diseases, making them the world's leading cause of death and accounting for 25% of global mortality. Contributing to this impact was the growing resistance of many vectors to pesticides and of some parasites to medicines, as well as the slow development of affordable new vaccines.

Vectors

A vector is an animal, typically an arthropod (e.g. a tick or insect), which transmits an infectious disease to a host. Most vectors acquire a disease from one host and transmit it to another. However, some vectors are infected 'vertically' via their mothers.

Environmental change plays a major role in the emergence and re-emergence of infectious diseases. For example, the deterioration or destruction of natural habitats can reduce the number of natural predators, change the dominance of species, or create favourable conditions for disease hosts. Infrastructure, such as dams and irrigation channels, creates ideal environments for mosquitoes, which are the vector responsible for diseases like malaria and dengue fever.

Diseases carried by agents that are outside the human host during most of their lifecycle are especially susceptible to being affected by environmental conditions.

Land use change and deforestation can bring people closer to wildlife, allowing previously unknown diseases to spread to humans. Ebola and Lyme disease are examples, but other diseases also have one or more animal reservoirs in the wild. The vast majority of emerging infectious diseases are *zoonotic*.

Zoonotic diseases

Zoonotic diseases are diseases in which the pathogen is transmitted from a non-human vertebrate host to humans.

Many people worldwide lack adequate sanitation, waste management or vector control. In 2012, 863 million people lived in slum-like conditions. Whether overcrowding results from poverty, or displacement due to conflicts or natural disasters, it can lead to contagion – creating a breeding ground for infectious diseases like influenza, malaria and West Nile virus that are carried by water, air, food, mosquitoes or rodents.

Read more about emerging and re-emerging infectious diseases in the 2004/5 Year Book.

© Balazs Kovacs Images/Shutterstock

Combatting infectious disease while addressing environmental challenges

Infectious diseases are the world's leading cause of death for children and adolescents. They are the second leading overall cause of death after heart disease. Continuous outbreaks of infectious diseases have been reported during the past decade. In the first half of 2014, ebola caused over 200 deaths in West Africa and over 500 people contracted Middle East Respiratory Syndrome (MERS). There were more than 145 fatal cases of MERS.

Although great strides have been made, millions of people continue to die each year from infectious diseases and millions more suffer permanent disabilities or poor health. A triple threat is represented by new infectious diseases, the re-emergence of infectious diseases that were once under control, and the continuous development of antibiotic resistance. Along with changes in society and technology – and in the microorganisms themselves – these factors are contributing to a 'perfect storm' of vulnerability.

Environmental factors play a major role in the development and transmission of infectious diseases. Science increasingly shows that human-induced changes in the environment linked to population dynamics, climate change, land use and globalization are associated with infectious disease patterns. Biodiversity, which can play an important role as a buffer, helps protect against infectious diseases. Several studies have suggested that as biodiversity is lost, there is an increase in the rate of disease transmission. A range of factors may be involved, including changes in the abundance and altered behaviour of a host, vector or parasite. This effect of biodiversity loss has been reported for diseases including malaria, Lyme disease, Chagas disease, leishmaniasis and schistosomiasis.

Major progress in malaria control in the past decade has also been made partly through environmental management. By preventing or removing the breeding sites of mosquitoes that carry the malaria parasite, and keeping the mosquitoes out of living spaces (e.g. with screens and treated mosquito bed nets, coupled with spraying), malaria transmission has been reduced to close to zero in some communities. Mortality rates dropped by 42% globally and by 49% in Africa between 2000 and 2012, with an estimated 450,000 lives saved in a single year.

However, global *climate change* is expected to result in increased rainfall and higher temperatures. It also will lead to changes in habitats and in the presence of vectors such as mosquitoes, which will be able to move into new areas and reach vulnerable populations that have had little or no previous exposure to the diseases. A recent study in the highlands of Ethiopia and Colombia showed that malaria is already spreading in warmer years to higher elevations where it was not previously seen. This implies that there may be further exposures of densely populated regions of Africa and Latin America to malaria as a result of climate change.

Preventing infectious diseases through environmental management and climate change mitigation is highly cost-effective. For example, malaria costs Africa US$12 billion annually while a comprehensive African malaria control programme would cost an average of US$3 billion per year.

Understanding how a changing climate and environment drive the emergence and re-emergence of infectious diseases can lead to effective strategies to combat their development and spread. Ecosystem- and community-based approaches have proven to be valuable tools.

Climate change: a game changer?

Climate change has implications for human health, especially with respect to vector-borne and water-borne infectious diseases such as cholera and dengue. Parasites and water-borne pathogens and vectors may find a more hospitable environment not only where there are warmer temperatures, but also where there is rising humidity or disaster events are occurring. In countries where some infectious diseases have essentially been eradicated, climate change could expand vector range and some diseases could make a comeback.

Taking actions to combat infectious diseases

The effectiveness of ecosystem and environmental management approaches in fighting the spread of infectious diseases is gaining recognition from governments and local communities. For example, a new project in Central America is taking an 'ecohealth approach' to combatting *Chagas disease* in El Salvador, Guatemala and Honduras. Researchers are working to reduce the transmission of this disease by controlling the insect species that infest poorly constructed homes and carry the disease-causing parasite. This project builds on the success of previous efforts in Guatemala (2003-10), where Chagas disease was controlled by combining community education with housing improvements.

Chagas disease

Chagas disease is one of the most serious public health challenges in Latin America and the Caribbean. It is caused by a parasite transmitted from wildlife or domestic animals to people by the bite of a triatomine bug. More than 10 million people in the region are infected with this disease, which is endemic in many poor, rural areas. One-third of those who are infected develop chronic Chagas. It kills more than 10,000 people per year.

Important messages about disease transmission need to be disseminated to communities in simple but innovative ways. Educational campaigns by non-governmental organizations (NGOs) and others help raise awareness and change community health and sanitation practices. In India a campaign promoting hand-washing with soap, SupperAmma, has brought about long-lasting behavioural changes in mothers and children that have helped reduce the rate of diarrhoea and respiratory infections.

Improving a community's access to water, sanitation and hygiene (WASH) is another effective way to minimize the risks of infectious disease. In 2012, WASH initiatives implemented through the United Nations Children's Fund (UNICEF) non-emergency programmes helped more than 10 million people gain access to improved sanitation, largely thanks to the expansion of community approaches. Such activities are also actively supported by NGOs and other UN organizations, including the United Nations Development Programme (UNDP), WHO and Oxfam.

Effective prevention of infectious diseases requires global cooperation and coordination. International travel and trade contribute to the rapid spread of infectious diseases. Surveillance is therefore another important line of defence. At the international level, WHO has established the Global Outbreak Alert and Response Network (GOARN), which links medical institutions, organizations and networks around the world to provide rapid identification of any outbreaks that might be of international importance. HealthMap is an innovative surveillance network established by a team of researchers, epidemiologists and software developers. Its freely accessible website uses data from traditional and public health information systems including online news, eyewitness and official reports, to provide real-time online surveillance information on emerging diseases. There is evidence that HealthMap increases the sensitivity and timeliness of alerts and reduces false alarms.

There were almost 7 billion mobile phone subscriptions globally in 2014. Mobile phones have the potential to support informal infectious disease surveillance networks in developing countries. An example is Alerta DISAMAR in Peru, which has received contributions from over 600 individuals and collected information on more than 80,000 cases and 31 disease outbreaks.

Roles of host species in the transmission of Lyme disease in the northeastern USA

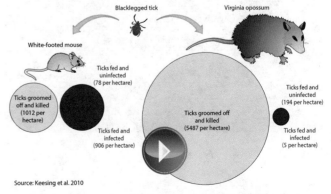

Blacklegged tick
Virginia opossum
White-footed mouse
Ticks fed and uninfected (78 per hectare)
Ticks groomed off and killed (1012 per hectare)
Ticks fed and infected (906 per hectare)
Ticks groomed off and killed (5487 per hectare)
Ticks fed and uninfected (194 per hectare)
Ticks fed and infected (5 per hectare)

Source: Keesing et al. 2010

For video links please go to http://www.archive.poughkeepsiejournal.com/article/20130303/NEWS04/303030062/VIDEO-Preservation-An-antidote-Lyme-disease

A multi-sectoral approach to ensure healthy life for all

The control of infectious diseases can be further strengthened through recognition of the potential contribution of environmental management to preventing their emergence and spread. Climate change remains one of the biggest threats with respect to the spread of vectors and water-borne disease, especially diarrhoeal diseases. Evidence, and better understanding, of the multiple benefits of climate change mitigation are growing. In addition, practical initiatives such as ensuring adequate access to safe water and sanitation (e.g. through the Sanitation and Water for All Global Partnership) and appropriate shelter contribute to combatting infectious diseases. International dialogue and cooperation have been essential in the past and will continue to be required in the future.

There is increasing recognition of the role ecosystems and biodiversity play in protecting and enhancing human health. This goes beyond undiscovered plants that might provide new treatments, or undisturbed wetlands that filter disease-causing organisms (e.g. in drinking water) – although these benefits are also important arguments for biodiversity conservation.

© Sanitation for All

Environmental disruption leads to the emergence, amplification and spread of new diseases, while intact ecosystems have a protective effect. This suggests an exciting new approach to infectious disease control: by working to ensure a strong and healthy environment, we can help protect people against the devastating impacts of infectious disease. There are formidable challenges to be met. Interactions within ecosystems are complex. However, there is much to be gained by pursuing this approach, which can supplement more traditional public health activities.

Like other urgent environmentally related problems (e.g. air and water pollution), infectious diseases know no boundaries. Efforts to prevent, detect and respond to infectious diseases cannot be carried out successfully at the local or national level alone, or by a single group of stakeholders. Combatting their spread requires well coordinated actions, based on reliable information and effective communication among various partners. Multi-sectoral approaches that recognize the roles of actors at all levels need to be better recognized and supported, particularly in developing countries, in order to address the links between human health, the environment and economic activities and make healthy lives for all possible.

© Shutterstock/tomgigabite

Further information about infectious diseases

Altizer, S., et al. (2013) Climate Change and Infectious Diseases: From Evidence to a Predictive Framework (abstract) http://www.sciencemag.org/content/341/6145/514.abstract

Batterman, S., et al. (2009) Sustainable Control of Water-Related Infectious Diseases: A Review and Proposal for Interdisciplinary Health-Based Systems Research. Environmental Health Perspectives, 117, 7, 1023-1032

Bezirtzoglou, C., et al. (2011) Climate changes, environment and infection: facts, scenarios and growing awareness from the public health community within Europe. Anaerobe, 17, 6, 337-40 http://www.sciencedirect.com/science/article/pii/S1075996411001053

Brownstein, J.S., et al. (2008). Surveillance Sans Frontières: Internet-Based Emerging Infectious Disease Intelligence and the HealthMap Project. PLOS Medicine, 8 July http://www.plosmedicine.org/article/info%3Adoi%2F10.1371%2Fjournal.pmed.0050151

CDC (Centers for Disease Control and Prevention) (United States) (2014a). Severe Acute Respiratory Syndrome (SARS) http://www.cdc.gov/sars/index.html

CDC (2014). West Nile Virus http://www.cdc.gov/westnile/index.html

CDC (2014). Ebola Hemorrhagic Fever. Outbreak of Ebola in Guinea, Liberia, and Sierra Leone http://www.cdc.gov/vhf/ebola/outbreaks/guinea/

CDC (2014). Middle East Respiratory Syndrome (MERS) http://www.cdc.gov/coronavirus/mers/

De Groot, B.R.J., et al. (2013) Middle East respiratory syndrome coronavirus (MERS-CoV): announcement of the Coronavirus Study Group. Journal Virol 2013; 87: 7790-7792 http://jvi.asm.org/content/87/14/7790.full

Ferro, J. (2013). Biodiversity impacts Lyme Disease. Poughkeepsie Journal, Feb. 28, 2013 http://www.poughkeepsiejournal.com/article/20130228/NEWS04/130228009/Coming-Sunday-Biodiversity-impacts-Lyme-disease-watch-video

Goldstein, B., et al. (2005). Emerging and Re-emerging Infectious Diseases: Links to Environmental Change. Geo Year Book (2004/2005) Emerging Challenges - New Findings http://www.unep.org/yearbook/2004/pdf/geo_yearbook_2004.pdf

Harvard School of Public Health/Centre for Health and the Global Environment (2012). Biodiversity and Infectious Diseases http://chge.med.harvard.edu/topic/biodiversity-and-infectious-diseases

IRDC (International Development Research Centre) (2014). Ecosystems and human health: Why we do what we do. http://www.idrc.ca/EN/Programs/Agriculture_and_the_Environment/Ecosystem_Approaches_to_Human_Health/Pages/About.aspx

IRDC (2014b). Ecosystems and human health: Tackling Chagas disease in Central America http://www.idrc.ca/en/programs/agriculture_and_the_environment/ecosystem_approaches_to_human_health/pages/articledetails.aspx?publicationid=1100

ITU (International Telecommunication Union) (2014). Mobile subscriptions near the 7 billion mark Does almost everyone have a phone? https://itunews.itu.int/En/3741-Mobile-subscriptions-near-the-78209billion-markbrDoes-almost-everyone-have-a-phone.note.aspx

Keesing, F., et al. (2010). Impacts of biodiversity on the emergence and transmission of infectious diseases. Nature

Levy, S. (2013) The Lyme Disease Debate Host Biodiversity and Human Disease Risk. Environmental Health Perspectives, 121, 4, a120–a125 http://www.ncbi.nlm.nih.gov/pmc/articles/PMC3620092/

Morand, S.S., et al. (2014). Infectious Diseases and Their Outbreaks in Asia-Pacific: Biodiversity and Its Regulation Loss Matter. PLoS One, 9, 2, e90032 http://www.plosone.org/article/info%3Adoi%2F10.1371%2Fjournal.pone.0090032

Myers, S.S., et al. (2013). Human health impacts of ecosystem alteration. Proceedings of the National Academy of Science, 110, 47, 18753-18760 http://www.wcs.org/files/pdfs/PNAS-2013-Human-health-impacts-of-ecosystem-alteration.pdf

Myers, S.S. and Patz, J.A. (2009). Emerging threats to human health from global environmental change. Annual Review of Environment and Resources, 34, 1. 223-252 http://chge.med.harvard.edu/sites/default/files/Myers_Emerging_Threats_To_Human_%20Health_from_%20Global_Environmental_Change.pdf

Ostfeld, R., and Keesing, F. (2012) Effects of host diversity on infectious disease. Annual Review Ecology, Evolution and Systematics, 43, 157-82 http://www.annualreviews.org/doi/abs/10.1146/annurev-ecolsys-102710-145022

Pongsiri, M. J., et al. (2009). Biodiversity Loss Affects Global Disease Ecology. BioScience, 59, 11, 945-954 http://www.epa.gov/ncer/biodiversity/pubs/bio_2009_59_11.pdf

Public Health Agency of Canada (2014). Frequently Asked Questions. Middle East Respiratory Syndrome Coronavirus (MERS-CoV) http://www.phac-aspc.gc.ca/eri-ire/coronavirus/fact-feuillet-eng.php

Randolph, S.E. (2009) Perspectives on climate change impacts on infectious diseases. Ecology, 90, 4, 927-931 http://www.esajournals.org/doi/abs/10.1890/08-0506.1

Siraj, A.S. (2014). Altitudinal Changes in Malaria Incidence in Highlands of Ethiopia and Colombia. Science, 343, 6175,1154-1158. http://www.sciencemag.org/content/343/6175/1154

The Global Health Policy Center (2014). Infectious Diseases: a Persistent Threat .http://www.smartglobalhealth.org/issues/entry/infectious-diseases

Ulery, B.D., et al. (2011). Design of a Protective Single-Dose Intranasal Nanoparticle-Based Vaccine Platform for Respiratory Infectious Diseases. PLoS ONE, 6,3, e17642 http://www.plosone.org/article/info%3Adoi%2F10.1371%2Fjournal.pone.0017642

UNICEF (United Nations Children's Fund) (2014). Sanitation updates. News, opinions and resources for sanitation for all http://sanitationupdates.wordpress.com

WHO (World Health Organization) (2003). SARS Outbreak Controlled. Worldwide Media Centre http://www.who.int/mediacentre/news/releases/2003/pr56/en/

WHO (2013). Global Vaccine Action Plan 2011-2020 http://www.who.int/immunization/global_vaccine_action_plan/GVAP_Introduction_and_Immunization_Landscape_Today.pdf?ua=1

WHO (2014). Ebola Virus Disease. Fact sheet N°103 http://www.who.int/mediacentre/factsheets/fs103/en/

WHO (2014). Health Topics. Emerging Disease Definition http://www.who.int/topics/emerging_diseases/en/

WHO (2014). Lyme Borreliosis (Lyme disease) http://www.who.int/ith/diseases/lyme/en/

WHO (2014). Global Alert and Response (GAR). MERS-CoV summary updates http://www.who.int/csr/disease/coronavirus_infections/archive_updates/en/

WHO (2014). Global Alert and Response (GAR). Poliomyelitis http://www.who.int/csr/don/archive/disease/poliomyelitis/en/

Yasuoka, J., et al. (2006). Impact of education on knowledge, agricultural practices, and community actions for mosquito control and mosquito-borne disease prevention in rice ecosystems in Sri Lanka. American Journal of Tropical Medicine and Hygiene, 74,6, 1034-1042 http://www.ajtmh.org/content/74/6/1034.full.pdf

UNEP Year Book 2014 emerging issues update

Fish and Shellfish Farming in Marine Ecosystems

Implications for the environment of providing food from the ocean

Helping to feed a growing world population, aquaculture production has increased since the 1950s from 650 thousand tonnes to almost 67 million tonnes. In the same period, the total marine catch has increased from 20 million to about 80 million tonnes. Today, aquaculture provides half of all fish for human consumption and the sector is expected to grow.

While significant progress has been made over the past decades towards making marine aquaculture more sustainable, environmental concerns remain – reflecting this sector's rapid growth. Broadly speaking, fish farms can release nutrients, undigested feed and veterinary drugs, and other biocides to the environment. They can also create conditions that increase risks of diseases and parasites and of harmful algal blooms. In some countries certain forms of shrimp farming have destroyed large areas of coastal habitats, such as mangrove forests. Farmed fish and shellfish can escape to surrounding waters, which may have negative impacts on ecosystems through genetic regression or introduction of invasive species. Use of fish-based feeds in aquaculture can put additional pressures on poorly managed wild fish stocks and on the marine environment.

Despite these implications for the environment, there is increasing potential for responsibly managed marine aquaculture to provide food from the oceans, particularly in view of increasing pressures on freshwater and terrestrial ecosystems, including those related to climate change. The main systems of marine aquaculture differ in their potential environmental consequences:

Extractive aquaculture is the practice of enhancing production of molluscs. Larvae or juveniles are seeded to the sea bottom or attached to manmade structures, where they grow feeding on (or 'extracting') natural phytoplankton. The detrimental environmental impacts of extractive aquaculture are comparatively low, partly because of the species' low *trophic level*. However, there is a risk that non-native species will be introduced.

Trophic level

The trophic level (TL) of a species is the number of consumption steps between that species and primary producers such as algae, which are by definition TL1. A filter feeding mussel has a TL between 2 and 3, while an Atlantic salmon is between TL4 and 5. To grow to the same weight a mussel requires less energy input than a salmon.

Shrimp farming has expanded rapidly in the past several decades. Destruction of coastal habitats, especially mangrove forests, has been attributed in particular to extensive shrimp farming. Other impacts include water pollution by chemicals and pharmaceuticals, eutrophication resulting from releases of nutrients in the form of feed and waste, and salinization of arable land and freshwater supplies. In many places there have also been social and community impacts.

Marine net pen farming involves rearing fish from the juvenile to harvest stages in net pens. Atlantic salmon is normally farmed in net pens. Environmental impacts include the discharge of waste to bottom-dwelling communities (e.g. cold water corals). The high density of Atlantic salmon in open cages can lead to disease or parasite outbreaks, with potential impacts on wild populations. Escapees can act as vectors and, particularly if genetically modified, affect wild populations' genetic variability. Marine net pen farmed species, which tend to feed naturally on fish, require high amounts of protein as well as fishmeal and fish oil in their diet. This can impact both terrestrial and marine ecosystems.

Read more about fish and shellfish farming in the 2006 Year Book.

Development of marine aquaculture

Marine aquaculture production has grown by over 35% since 2004 in total volume. Farmed fish production surpassed beef production in 2012. In absolute terms, the greatest growth in fish and shellfish farming has been in Asia. The highest relative growth has taken place in Oceania. While the economic importance of marine aquaculture in Small Island Developing States (SIDS) varies, it is low overall. Africa was expected to see a 'dramatic increase' in marine aquaculture over the past decade, but this increase has not been realized so far. With the decline in production of tiger shrimp, the size of the sector has shrunk in Africa.

Europe is the only region where the share of marine aquaculture in total aquaculture production is growing. To a great extent, this is due to successful farming of Atlantic salmon, one of the species with the highest production (2 million tonnes globally in 2012). Molluscs also continue to contribute a significant portion of production (over 20%).

Recently there has been notable growth in production of a number of aquaculture species, including groupers, milkfish, Indo-Pacific swamp crab, pompanos, turbot, sole and whiteleg shrimp. Production of whiteleg shrimp overtook that of tiger shrimp in 2003. It requires less expensive feed than tiger shrimp due to a lower protein requirement, and overall production costs are lower.

Fish feeds for carnivorous, high trophic level fish species typically contain large amounts of protein – often sourced from *fishmeal and fish oil* – with potentially detrimental effects on poorly managed wild fish stocks. Since production trophic level of fishmeal and fish oil is stabilizing and prices are rising, the aquaculture sector is seeking alternatives. In Norway, for example, the share of fishmeal, fish oil and plant protein in Atlantic salmon production changed from 64, 23 and 0% respectively in 1990 to 26, 17 and 37% in 2010. Overall, a decrease in the trophic level of cultured finfish was reported between 1950 and 2006, with a slight increase since the mid-1980s.

Aquaculture has been estimated to use 63 and 81%, respectively, of global fishmeal and fish oil. Fish feeds for carnivorous, high trophic fish species typically contain large amounts of protein – often sourced from fishmeal and fish oil – which could potentially have detrimental effects on poorly managed wild fish stocks. While their shares in feeds are decreasing due to replacement by alternative ingredients, fishmeal and fish oil will continue to be used to meet nutritional requirements but at lower levels. Fish processing offcuts have been identified as a potentially important source of high-quality feed ingredient and already provide 25% of all fishmeal and fish oil used. Alternatives should not be considered in isolation. For example, replacing fishmeal and fish oil with plants such as soy or rapeseed might have unwanted detrimental impacts on terrestrial ecosystems.

Another important development is the relocation of shrimp farms from tidal mangrove habitats to sites (and natural habitats) further upland, using more intensive production patterns requiring greater investments and technical expertise. According to the Global Aquaculture Alliance, today mangrove losses due to shrimp farming have virtually ceased to occur.

Fishmeal and fish oil

Immense populations of forage fish and low trophic species such as anchovy, herring and krill live in the ocean. They are often the cornerstones of marine food webs. So-called 'reduction fisheries' produce protein and nutrient-rich fishmeal and fish oil used as feed in aquaculture – where it can be indispensable – and for raising animals such as poultry. They are also increasingly used as direct human nutrition (e.g. in fish oil in capsules). The largest fishery in the world (for Peruvian anchovy) is a forage fishery where less than 1% of fish are used for human consumption.

Marine aquaculture with less impact

Consumer awareness of, and interest in, more sustainable aquaculture products is increasing. Sector-based activities such as the Global Salmon Initiative are important responsive mechanisms that can also support sustainability certification. A number of aquaculture related certification schemes have been developed in past years. They include Naturland, the Global Aquaculture Alliance (GAA) Best Aquaculture Practices (BAP) standards, and the Aquaculture Stewardship Council (ASC). The ASC has adopted standards for salmon as well as tilapia, pangasius, trout, abalone and bivalves. It adopted a shrimp standard in March 2014. Many farms have already been certified to these standards. The technical guidelines of the Food and Agriculture Organization (FAO) on aquaculture certification were recently approved at intergovernmental level.

Independent sustainability certification can be a powerful tool that goes beyond improvement of production standards and labeling of certain products to inform consumers. It can also bring about enhanced sector transparency and the provision of better information on impacts. Certification is an effective lever for further development of industry standards and governance mechanisms.

Integrated aquaculture is a practice that combines different kinds of aquaculture (e.g. fish, shellfish and seaweed cultivation) to minimize environmental impacts by creating balanced ecological systems in which, for example, shellfish and seaweeds filter excess nutrients produced by the fish while providing another economic mainstay. This approach is commonly practiced in freshwater environments, particularly in Asian carp farming, but its potential has yet to be realized in the marine environment. The use in aquaculture operations of offshore structures such as wind farms – which could reduce competition for space – is another approach with great potential.

Significant health related technological advances have taken place in marine aquaculture. For example, specific pathogen free tiger and whiteleg shrimp broodstock, or vaccinations of salmon, can reduce the need to use chemicals in farming for disease treatment with their associated environmental impacts. In net pens, wrasses have been used as cleaner fish to treat sea lice.

The increase in the number of closed aquaculture systems whose exchanges with natural ecosystems are limited, could potentially reduce the impacts of wastewater and chemicals from aquaculture on water quality.

The FAO has published an extensive series of technical guidelines which support the public and private sector in taking concrete steps to make marine aquaculture sustainable.

A significant global contribution to sustainability could be made by shifting from cultivation of high to lower trophic level species, particularly mussels. Further strengthening of the amount of sustainably produced plant ingredients in feeds would also help reduce marine aquaculture's environmental footprint.

© Thomas Bjørkan

Capitalizing on progress

As marine aquaculture has been experiencing rapid growth, significant technological advances have been made that address some of the sector's environmental impacts. The environmental footprint of aquaculture (including marine aquaculture) is likely to be lower than that of other protein production methods, depending on their particular impacts. However, due to continued growth overall environmental impacts from aquaculture are expected to at least double by 2030. While the private sector's role and responsibility to respond to marine aquaculture's environmental challenges will continue to be critical, governments remain key to promoting and stimulating sustainable practices.

Marine aquaculture cannot be seen as an isolated sector. Its management should be based on (and part of) overall ecosystem-based management, including the use of approaches such as marine spatial planning and environmental impact assessment. The FAO defines an ecosystem approach to aquaculture as 'a strategy for the integration of the activity within the wider ecosystem such that it promotes sustainable development, equity and resilience of interlinked social-ecological systems.' Thus, the involvement of sector and public stakeholders is critical for this approach's success.

Setting operational standards (e.g. for protecting coastal ecosystems or use of chemicals) is important to help ensure a level playing field across the sector. Technical regulations and targeted subsidies for investments in low-impact technology can be an incentive for more sustainable practices. While standards might have to be set nationally, international organizations such as FAO – as well as sector roundtables and non-governmental initiatives – should continue to facilitate progress, supported by capacity building and training initiatives that help the marine aquaculture industry develop and embrace best environmental practices.

Stricter regulation can also lead to innovation that drives down costs and impacts, as seen in farmed salmon production. This can be supported by targeted research to strengthen the operational and environmental knowledge base, and to shape cross-country and cross-sector learning networks.

Healthy marine ecosystems are fundamental to reaching development goals – not only with respect to securing food, but also to providing jobs. Marine aquaculture's current impacts and predicted growth call for continued and strengthened efforts towards environmentally sound development of the sector to avoid the loss of important ecosystem services. Technical innovations, the experience and growing skills of aquaculture producers, and improved knowledge of environmental impacts and operational and governance opportunities provide reasons to hope for a sustainable marine aquaculture sector supporting a growing world population with food and livelihoods.

© JoeLena/iStock

For video links please go to http://www.youtube.com/watch?v=zpAvBeZnKiA

Further information about fish and shellfish farming

Bouwman, A.F., Pawlowski, M., Liu, C., Beusen, A.H.W., Shumway, S.E., Glibert, P.M. and Overbeek, C.C. (2011). Global Hindcasts and Future Projections of Coastal Nitrogen and Phosphorus Loads Due to Shellfish and Seaweed Aquaculture. Reviews in Fisheries Science, 19(4): 331-357

Bouwman, A.F., Beusen, A.H.W.; Gilbert, P.M; Overbeek, C.C., Pawlowski, M. Herrerra, Jorge; M., Sandor; Yu, R. and Zhou, M. (2013). Mariculture: significant and expanding cause of coastal nutrient enrichment. Environment research letters, 8(4): 1-5

Bouwman, A.F., Beusen, A.H.W., Overbeek, C.C., Bureau, D.P., Pawlowski, M. and Glibert, P.M. (2013). Hindcasts and Future Projections of Global Inland and Coastal Nitrogen and Phosphorus Loads Due to Finfish Aquaculture. Reviews in Fisheries Science, 21(2): 112-156

Chamberlain, A. (2011). Fishmeal and fish oil - The facts, figures, trends and IFFO's responsible supply standard http://www.iffo.net/system/files/FMFOF2011_0.pdf

Earth Policy Institute (2013). Farmed Fish Production Overtakes Beef http://www.earth-policy.org/plan_b_updates/2013/update114

Ecoplan International (EPI) (2008). Global assessment of closed system aquaculture http://www.davidsuzuki.org/publications/downloads/2008/Closed-System-Aquac-Global-Review.pdf

Environmental Justice Foundation (EJF) (2004). Farming The Sea, Costing The Earth: Why We Must Green The Blue Revolution http://www.ejfoundation.org/sites/default/files/public/farming_the_sea.pdf

FAO (Food and Agriculture Organization) (no date). Cultured Aquatic Species Information Programme: Penaeus vannamei http://www.fao.org/fishery/culturedspecies/Litopenaeus_vannamei/en

FAO (2008). The potential of spatial planning tools to support the ecosystem approach to aquaculture http://www.fao.org/docrep/012/i1359e/i1359e00.htm

FAO (2009). Impact of rising feed ingredient prices on aquafeeds and aquaculture production http://www.fao.org/docrep/012/i1143e/i1143e00.htm

FAO (2009). Integrated mariculture. A global review http://www.fao.org/docrep/012/i1092e/i1092e00.htm

FAO (2009). Environmental impacts assessment and monitoring in aquaculture http://www.fao.org/docrep/012/i0970e/i0970e00.htm

FAO (2010). World Aquaculture 2010 http://www.fao.org/docrep/014/ba0132e/ba0132e00.htm

FAO (2010). Aquaculture Development 4. Ecosystem approach to aquaculture http://www.fao.org/docrep/013/i1750e/i1750e00.htm

FAO (2011). Technical Guidelines on Aquaculture Certification http://www.fao.org/docrep/015/i2296t/i2296t00.pdf

FAO (2012). Farming the waters for people and food http://www.fao.org/fishery/nems/40153/en

FAO (2013). FAO Aquaculture Information Products http://www.fao.org/fishery/aquaculture/information-products/en

FAO (2013). Expanding mariculture farther offshore – Technical, environmental, spatial and governance challenges. FAO Technical Workshop. 22-25 March 2010. Orbetello, Italy (Lovatelli, A., Aguilar-Manjarrez, J., and Soto, D., eds) http://www.fao.org/docrep/018/i3092e/i3092e00.htm

FAO (2014). The State of World Fisheries and Aquaculture http://www.fao.org/fishery/sofia/en

FAO (2014). Data for marine environment, crustaceans, molluscs and all fish species 1950-2012 http://www.fao.org/fishery/statistics/global-aquaculture-production/query/en

Global Agriculture Alliance (GAA) (2011). Mangroves http://www.gaalliance.org/newsroom/whitepapers-detail.php?Mangroves-12

Hall, S.J., et al. (2011). Blue Frontiers: Managing the Environmental Costs of Aquaculture http://www.worldfishcenter.org/resource_centre/media/pdfs/blue_frontiers/report.pdf

Nofima (2011). Today's and tomorrow's feed ingredients in Norwegian aquaculture http://www.nofima.no/en/publication/3A106947AA44C668C125799100336E38

Stokstad, E. (2010). Down on the Shrimp Farm. Science, 328, 1504-1505 http://www.researchgate.net/publication/44683419_Down_on_the_shrimp_farm

Tacon, A.G.J. and Metian, M. (2008). Global overview on the use of fish meal and fish oil in industrially compounded aquafeeds: Trends and future prospects. Aquaculture, 285, 146-158 http://www.sciencedirect.com/science/article/pii/S004484860800567X

Tacon, A.G.J., et al. (2010). Responsible Aquaculture and Trophic Level Implications to Global Fish Supply. Reviews in Fisheries Science, 18, 1, 94-105 http://www.researchgate.net/publication/233078215_Responsible_Aquaculture_and_Trophic_Level_Implications_to_Global_Fish_Supply

UNEP (2006). Fish and shellfish farming in marine ecosystems. In: GEO Year Book 2006 http://www.unep.org/yearbook/2006

World Bank (2013). Fish to 2030: Prospects for Fisheries and Aquaculture http://www.fao.org/docrep/019/i3640e/i3640e.pdf

UNEP Year Book 2014 emerging issues update

Illegal Trade in Wildlife

The high environmental, social and economic costs

At the start of the 20th century Africa was home to an estimated million black rhinos belonging to four sub-species. By 2007 there were fears that the Western black rhino, with its distinctive dexterous upper lip, had become extinct, while the number of wild northern white rhino had never been lower. Levels of poaching and illegal trade in ivory, which had fallen in the 1990s, began to rise again with an unprecedented spike in illegal trade of elephant tusks and rhinoceros horns.

Demand for illegal wildlife products is based on their use in traditional East Asian medicine, the international trade in commercial goods (e.g. timber) and exotic pets, and a desire for status symbols, among other factors. Illegal trade in animals, plants (including timber and charcoal) and fish is one of the largest sources of criminal earnings in the world – ranking alongside trafficking of drugs, people and arms. Today illegal wildlife trade is estimated to be worth US$50-150 billion per year. The global illegal fisheries catch is valued at US$10-23.5 billion a year and illegal logging, including processing, at US$30-100 billion.

Numbers like these do not even begin to capture the environmental, social and economic costs of illegal wildlife trade, which hinder investments in tourism and other types of development as well as threatening the ecosystems and biodiversity on which economic development often depends. Widespread failure of forest governance, characterized by illegal logging, associated illegal trade, and corruption, undermines attempts to achieve sustainable economic growth, social balance and environmental protection.

Profits from the illegal wildlife trade are often used to finance further illegal activity, including other forms of *transnational organized crime*. Loss of species can have devastating consequences. As an example, elephants are 'ecological engineers'. They change the landscape by uprooting grasses and trees, stripping bark and dispersing the seeds of the forage they eat, helping to create rich and diverse environments. The resulting biodiverse ecosystems not only support humans with food and other resources – and make

Transnational organized crime

Illegal wildlife trade is often carried out by criminal groups operating across borders. They are attracted by high profits and low risks associated with weak governance and lax penalties. International cooperation and mutual legal assistance among countries can help prevent, combat and eradicate such trafficking. National law enforcement and legal frameworks, and the UN Convention against Transnational Organized Crime (which entered into force in 2003) and its protocols, all have an important role to play in this regard.

environmentally sustainable tourism activities possible –they are also more resilient in the face of threats from e.g. diseases or extreme weather.

While the resurgence of illegal wildlife trade has become more evident, there is also better understanding of the impact of globalization, with illegal trade connecting producers and consumers around the world. The expansion of economies, international commerce, transportation, and the use of information and communication technology (ICT) help fuel demands for illegal wildlife products. To control such environmental crime, strong, international and coordinated governance is essential. The UN Commission on Crime Prevention and Criminal Justice adopted in 2007 a resolution on international cooperation in preventing and combatting illicit international trafficking in forest products, including timber, wildlife and other forest biological resources.

Read more about globalization and the environment in the 2007 Year Book.

Recognition of illegal wildlife trade as a serious crime

Illegal wildlife trade is no longer an emerging issue: the numbers tell the story. Today more elephants are being slaughtered than at any time in the past 20 years. Officials have estimated that close to 25,000 elephants were killed in 2013 to supply the illegal ivory trade, with ivory reportedly priced at over US$2200 per kg on the streets of Beijing, China. Over the past few years, the number of elephants killed annually has doubled compared to 2007. For the rhinoceros the statistics are even more bleak. Over 1000 were slaughtered in 2013 in South Africa, more than any other single year. Between 2007 and 2013, rhino poaching increased by 7000% in South Africa. Rhino horn, with its supposed but unproven medicinal qualities, can bring over US$66,000 per kg on the black market. About 20,000 white rhinos and 4880 black rhinos remained in the wild as of February 2013.

Organized crime is attracted by the possibility of huge profits with little risk, and penalties that are both disproportionately small and not always enforced. However, local communities may suffer most from the presence of violent gangs as well as the deterioration of the environment. Two iconic species, rhino and elephant, are threatened with extinction because of the illegal wildlife trade, driven by growing demand primarily from South East Asia and China.

Trends in illegal logging are also rising. Illegally logged timber from East Asia and the Pacific, which ends up in furniture and homes around the world, accounts for a staggering US$17 billion a year – an amount equal to the value of illegal trafficking of people, drugs and counterfeit goods in this region. In Africa, evidence is growing that illegal charcoal trade is linked to threat finance.

Encouraged by poverty, poorly monitored borders, corruption, and weak regulations and enforcement, wildlife poaching and trafficking continue to grow. The supply chain from producer to consumer involves more people in more countries (including some police, customs officers, and legal and political figures) as illegal products are transported using sophisticated smuggling techniques and routes. Reports

that rebel armies use money obtained through the illegal ivory trade to buy guns and ammunition illustrate the impact this activity can have on both local stability within countries and international security. In January 2014, the UN Security Council adopted two resolutions sanctioning wildlife trafficking, primarily designed to target armed rebel groups that use the illegal ivory trade as a way to generate finances.

While the problem continues to worsen, the international community is becoming increasingly focused on wildlife crime, recognizing the seriousness of its environmental, social and economic impacts. The fundamental institution regulating wildlife trade, the Convention on International Trade in Endangered Species of Wild Fauna and Flora (CITES), was strengthened at its last Conference of the Parties in 2013, when over 200 timber species and a variety of marine animals (e.g. sharks, manta rays, turtles) were added to the protected species list. In April 2013, the UN Commission on Crime Prevention and Criminal Justice sought to toughen existing laws by declaring wildlife trafficking a 'serious crime' with offences carrying a minimum penalty of four years of imprisonment.

© UNEP Sudan Environmental Database

Are we turning a corner? Small steps towards success

The crisis is real, but there are hopeful signs that with cooperative efforts and planning innovative solutions can be found to disrupt the illegal wildlife trade. The international community is coming together to make a stronger, more unified effort to fight back.

However, the supply chain is highly complex, crossing many borders. There are links connecting poachers in source countries, transnational criminal syndicates, and traders and consumers in East Asia, Europe, North America and elsewhere. The international police organization INTERPOL and the UN Office on Drugs and Crime (UNODC) have begun to assess patterns and cross-overs between illegal wildlife trade and other serious crime, such as drug smuggling and money laundering, and to apply lessons learned in these areas.

Although weak laws and local corruption give criminals escape routes, emerging international law and policing efforts – in partnership with communities and countries – are producing some exciting results. Early in 2014, 28 countries and environmental and law enforcement agencies worked together for a month on a sting operation known as 'Cobra Two'. It netted 36 rhino horns, more than three tonnes of ivory, over a thousand skins of endangered animals, and hundreds of tonnes of logs from protected trees. This groundbreaking operation also resulted in more than 400 arrests in Asia and Africa.

Customs officials play a vital role in apprehending illegal material at borders. The World Customs Organization (WCO) works to ensure that customs enforcement operations act to determine the legitimacy of all goods being declared for entry or exit. Rigorous and increased inspection and border control along with increased sharing of communication and co-operation between regions, countries and organizations involved in fighting illegal wildlife trade could help pick up illegal products as they move from source to purchaser.

Collaboration between international organizations has resulted in another major advance in the fight against illegal wildlife trade, with the formation of the International Consortium on Combating Wildlife Crime (ICCWC). Composed of the CITES Secretariat, INTERPOL, UNODC, the World Bank and WCO, the ICCWC was created to ensure a strong and co-ordinated response to wildlife crime. In 2012 it developed the Wildlife and Forest Crime Analytical Toolkit to assist governments in identifying the strengths and weaknesses of their criminal justice responses to wildlife and forest crime. Today the ICCWC is recognized as the world's leading intergovernmental initiative in the fight against wildlife crime.

Enforcement efforts are taking advantage of the latest technology for detection, analysis and communication. Monitoring and data collection through the Wildlife Enforcement Monitoring System (WEMS), for example, helps African countries to track illegal wildlife trade, monitor legal enforcement, capture trends, and share the information among participants. In pilot projects, drones equipped with video cameras are being used to keep a 'virtual eye' on rhinos and Bengal tigers in inaccessible areas of Chitwan National Park in Nepal. The volume of internationally traded products such as timber and fish from certified sources is small but growing. The latest technology, such as DNA and isotope analyses, can be used to increase and improve monitoring of wildlife products, their origins, destinations and transboundary movements.

Awareness raising campaigns, social media and marketing are being used to address the final link in the supply chain – consumer demand. The majority of ivory and rhino horn consumers reside in Asia, where a wealthier middle class now sees ivory as affordable. In the case of timber products and fish, consumers may live almost anywhere in the world. Misinformation and lack of understanding about the scale of illegal wildlife trade, how these products are obtained and the trade's impacts, lead to poorly informed decisions. Therefore, education is of key importance. Many awareness-raising initiatives have been launched by non-governmental organizations (NGOs) and others to profile the issues. The use of social media is building momentum as an effective and efficient global way to educate and reduce the demand for illegal wildlife products. Celebrities are particularly influential in their ability to break through the clutter and reach large and diverse audiences.

Combatting illegal wildlife trade through international collaboration

Illegal wildlife trade must be controlled. It threatens the environment, deprives communities of their livelihoods, decreases revenues for governments and businesses, and increases the probability of conflicts creating security risks – in addition to jeopardizing the survival of some species.

The key to success in the fight against illegal wildlife trade is collaboration among countries and international agencies. Efficient control of transboundary movements of wildlife products requires good information exchange and cooperation, involving importing, exporting and transit countries. Mechanisms need to be enhanced to facilitate rapid exchanges of intelligence between enforcement agencies.

Illegal wildlife trade still has a relatively low priority compared to other transnational crimes such as drug smuggling, human trafficking or counterfeit products. As the routes used to transport illegal wildlife products are the same as those used for drugs, people and weapons, successful approaches in these areas need to be considered to combat illegal wildlife. A protocol on environmental crime under the Convention on Transboundary Crime might provide a regulatory framework for doing this.

As regulations are only as good as their enforcement, provisions for enforcement need to be strengthened, with clear mandates and roles, sufficient resources, and effective penalties to discourage illegal wildlife trade. Enforcement

© UNEP

could be incorporated and strengthened as an integral part of the implementation of multilateral environmental agreements (MEAs). In addition, more support needs to be given to enforcement agencies in countries, including inspectors, customs officers, police and the judiciary, such as training of personnel, promotion of cooperation to control transboundary movements of environmental goods, and investigation and prosecution of criminals.

Above all, educating communities in which there is a demand for illegal wildlife products is essential. Campaigns to change the public opinion are powerful tools for reducing this demand. Targeting communities where supplies originate, by providing increased training and education and offering alternative livelihoods, also needs to be part of the strategy. Ensuring the exchange of information, the traceability of goods and widespread knowledge in society of the scale and impact of illegal wildlife trade is paramount.

Five parts of the Wildlife and Forest Crime Analytic Toolkit

Source: Wildlife and Forest Crime Analytic Toolkit

For video links please go to https://www.youtube.com/watch?v=r0hgJnE5T1Y

illegal wildlife trade

Further information about illegal wildlife trade

Agnew, D.J., et al., (2009). Estimating the worldwide extent of illegal fishing. PloS One, 4, 2, e4570 http://dx.plos.org/10.1371/journal.pone.0004570

Akella, A.S. and Allan, C. (2012). Dismantling wildlife crime: executive summary www.traffic.org/general-pdfs/Dismantling-Wildlife-Crime.pdf

Anderson, L. (2014). Policy Update #1: International wildlife crime: An IISD Overview of Recent Events – Biodiversity Policy & Practice. IISD Reporting Service http://biodiversity-l.iisd.org/policy-updates/international-wildlife-crime-an-iisd-overview-of-recent-events/#ftn9

Campos-Arceiz, A. and Blake, S. (2011). Megagardeners of the forest – the role of elephants in seed dispersal. Acta Oecologica, 37, 6, pp.542-553 http://www.sciencedirect.com/science/article/pii/S1146609X11000154

Chandran, R., et al. (2013). Bytes beyond borders: strengthening transboundary information sharing on wildlife crime through the Wildlife Enforcement Monitoring System (WEMS) initiative http://archive.ias.unu.edu/resource_centre/bytes_beyond_borders-strengthening_transboundary_information.pdf

CITES (Convention on International Trade in Endangered Species of Wild Fauna and Flora) (2013). CITES conference takes decisive action to halt decline of tropical timber, sharks, manta rays and a wide range of other plants and animals. http://www.cites.org/eng/news/pr/2013/20130314_cop16.php

ENS (Environment News Service) (2014). Global Wildlife Crime Sting Arrests 400+ Suspects.http://ens-newswire.com/2014/02/17/global-wildlife-crime-sting-arrests-400-suspects/

Gómez, A. and Aguirre, A.A. (2008). Infectious diseases and the illegal wildlife trade. Annals of the New York Academy of Sciences, 1149, 16-19 http://www.ncbi.nlm.nih.gov/pubmed/19120165

Haynes, G. (2012). Elephants (and extinct relatives) as earth-movers and ecosystem engineers. Geomorphology, 157-158, 99-107 http://www.sciencedirect.com/science/article/pii/S0169555X1100314X

IFAW (International Fund for Animal Welfare) (n.d.). A case for stepping up CITES enforcement in the EUhttp://www.ifaw.org/united-states/resource-centre/ifaw-case-stepping-cites-enforcement-eu

IISD Reporting Services (2012). Summary of the World Congress on Justice, Governance and Law for Environmental Sustainability, 17-20 June 2012. UNEP World Congress Bulletin, 203,1 http://www.iisd.ca/download/pdf/sd/ymbvol203num1e.pdf

INTERPOL (2014). Executive Summary – Assessment of Enforcement Responses to Tiger Crime http://www.interpol.int/Media/Files/Crime-areas/Environmental-crime/Executive-Summary-Assessment-of-Enforcement-Responses-to-Tiger-Crime/

INTERPOL (2014). National Environmental Security Task Force – Bringing Compliance and Enforcement Agencies Together to Maintain Environmental Security http://www.interpol.int/en/Media/Files/Crime-areas/Environmental-crime/NEST/National-Environmental-Security-Task-Force-Manual-2012/

IUCN (International Union for Conservation of Nature) (n.d.) IUCN Red List of Threatened Species: Diceros bicornis ssp. longipes (Western Black Rhino, Western Black Rhinoceros) http://www.iucnredlist.org/details/39319/0

Lagrot, I., et al. (2008). Probable extinction of the western black rhino, Diceros bicornis longipes: 2006 survey in northern Cameroon. Pachyderm, 43, 19-28 http://www.pachydermjournal.org/index.php/pachy/article/view/64

Lawson, K. and Vines, A. (2014). Global Impact of the Illegal Wildlife Trade - The Costs of Crime, Insecurity and Institutional Erosion http://www.chathamhouse.org/sites/files/chathamhouse/public/Research/Africa/0214Wildlife.pdf

London Declaration on Illegal Wildlife Trade (2014). London Conference on the Illegal Wildlife Trade – Declaration https://www.gov.uk/government/uploads/system/uploads/attachment_data/file/281289/london-wildlife-conference-declaration-140213.pdf

Maisels, F., et al., (2013). Devastating decline of forest elephants in central Africa. PloS One, 8,3, e59469 http://dx.plos.org/10.1371/journal.pone.0059469

Monster, H.W. (2013.). Roundtable Discusses Wildlife Trafficking as National Security Issue http://southafrica.usembassy.gov/news20130510b.html

Nasseri, N.A., et al. (2011). The impact of tree modification by African elephant (Loxodonta africana) on herpetofaunal species richness in northern Tanzania. African Journal of Ecology, 49, 2, 133-140 http://doi.wiley.com/10.1111/j.1365-2028.2010.01238.x

Nyberg, R. (USAID) (2014). Conservationists Applaud Global Wildlife Protection Operation http://www.usaid.gov/asia-regional/press-releases/conservationists-applaud-global-wildlife-protection

Paramaguru, K. (2014). A Landmark International Agreement to Halt Wildlife Trafficking Is Just the Beginning. Time, 14 February. http://science.time.com/2014/02/14/a-landmark-international-agreement-to-halt-wildlife-trafficking-is-just-the-beginning/

Platt, J.R. (2013). How the Western Black Rhino Went Extinct. Extinction Countdown in Scientific American Blog Network http://blogs.scientificamerican.com/extinction-countdown/2013/11/13/western-black-rhino-extinct/

Rao, P. (2013). Elephants are the latest conflict resource. Africa Renewal Online, 27, 3, 28 http://www.un.org/africarenewal/magazine/december-2013/elephants-are-latest-conflict-resource

Scanlon, J.E. (2012). Guest Article #13: CITES: From Stockholm in '72 to Rio+20 - Back to the future – Sustainable Development Policy & Practice. IISD Reporting Services http://uncsd.iisd.org/guest-articles/cites-from-stockholm-in-'72-to-rio20-back-to-the-future

Scanlon, J.E. (2013). Guest Article #17: CITES CoP16, Bangkok 2013: A "Watershed Moment" for Combating Wildlife Crime - Biodiversity Policy & Practice. IISD Reporting Services http://biodiversity-l.iisd.org/guest-articles/cites-cop16-bangkok-2013-a-?watershed-moment?-for-combating-wildlife-crime/

Sonricker Hansen, A.L., et al. (2012). Digital surveillance: a novel approach to monitoring the illegal wildlife trade. PloS One, 7, 12, e51156 http://dx.plos.org/10.1371/journal.pone.0051156

UN/UNEP (2014). Illegal Trade in Wildlife: The Environmental, Social and Economic Consequences for Sustainable Development, 1-9 www.unep.org/unea/download.asp?ID=4732

UNEP/CITES/IUCN/TRAFFIC (2013). Elephants in the Dust – The African Elephant Crisis http://www.unep.org/pdf/RRAivory_draft7.pdf

UNEP (2007). Environment and Globalization: Minimizing Risks, Seizing Opportunities. In: GEO Year Book 2007, 43-60 http://www.unep.org/yearbook/2007/PDF/6_Feature_Focus72dpi.pdf

UNEP (2012). Green Carbon, Black Trade: Illegal Logging, Tax Fraud and Laundering in the Worlds Tropical Forests. A Rapid Response Assessment http://www.unep.org/pdf/RRAlogging_english_scr.pdf

UNEP (2013). New Forensic Technique May Help Track Illegal Ivory – UNEP http://www.unep.org/newscentre/Default.aspx?DocumentID=2723&ArticleID=9560&l=en

UNODC (UN Office on Drugs and Crime) (2013). Transnational Organized Crime in East Asia and the Pacific – A Threat Assessment http://www.unodc.org/documents/southeastasiaandpacific/Publications/2013/TOCTA_EAP_web.pdf

UNODC (2014). Wildlife crime worth USD 8-10 billion annually, ranking it alongside human trafficking, arms and drug dealing in terms of profits: UNODC chief http://www.unodc.org/unodc/en/frontpage/2014/May/wildlife-crime-worth-8-10-billion-annually.html?ref=fs4

Wyler, L.S. and Sheikh, P.A. (2013). International Illegal Trade in Wildlife: Threats and U.S. Policy http://www.fas.org/sgp/crs/misc/RL34395.pdf

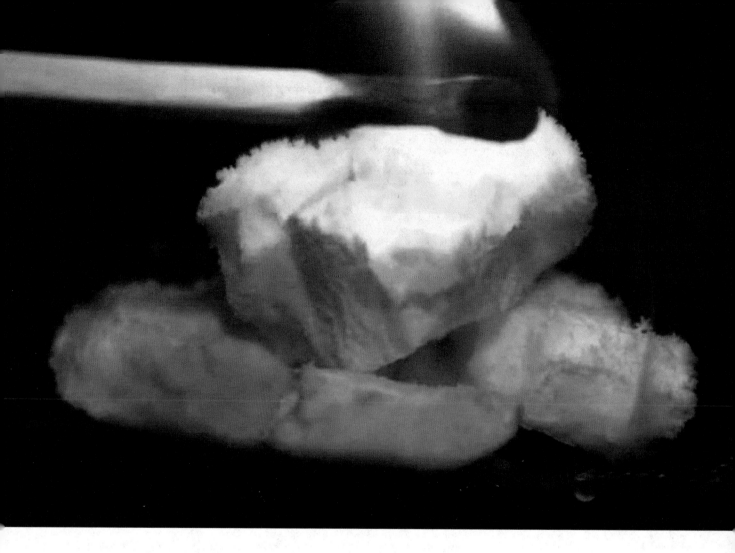

UNEP Year Book 2014 emerging issues update

Methane from Hydrates

Methane hydrates

There has been a surge of interest in methane hydrates in the last decade, stimulated by claims that their energy production potential could be larger than that of all the world's known oil and gas reserves combined. The reality is that the size of the global methane hydrate inventory is unknown.

What is known is that a vast reservoir of methane (CH_4) is frozen as methane hydrates. Methane hydrates are formed when high concentrations of methane and water combine at low temperatures and high pressures. Globally, an estimated 99% of all *gas hydrates* occur in the sediments of marine continental margins. The remainder are mainly found beneath Arctic permafrost. In the open ocean, where average bottom-water temperatures are approximately 2-4°C, gas hydrates are found starting at depths of around 500 metres.

Gas hydrates

Gas hydrates are ice-like substances formed when methane or some other gases combine with water at appropriate pressures and temperature conditions. Large amounts of methane are sequestered in gas hydrates. Those in which methane is sequestered are referred to as methane hydrates or methane clathrates.

Methane is a potent greenhouse gas with a considerably higher warming potential than carbon dioxide (CO_2). There are many natural and anthropogenic sources of methane emissions, including wetlands, ruminant animals, rice cultivation, deforestation, coal production, incomplete fossil fuel combustion, and the production and distribution of petroleum and natural gas. Methane is the main component of natural gas.

Methane hydrates destabilize in response to warming of only a few degrees Celsius. Therefore, some scientists are concerned about how much methane could potentially be released to the atmosphere from destabilized methane hydrates as a result of global warming. If this methane did

General schematic showing typical modes of gas hydrate occurrence relative to the geologic environment

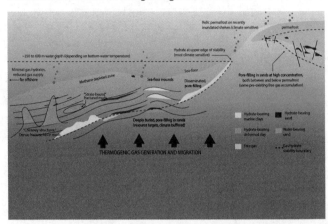

Source: R. Boswell 2011 adapted by GRID-Arendal

reach the atmosphere, it would in turn exacerbate global warming. However, most hydrates are in very deep oceans well within the gas hydrate stability field. Hydrates located in certain places close to the edge of the stability field could be a greater cause for concern.

A number of factors influence the extent to which methane hydrates-based natural gas production could eventually provide some countries with greater energy self-sufficiency and help address global energy needs. An important one is the global energy mix in years to come. As yet, no long-term production test has been carried out to demonstrate the viability of sustained methane production from gas hydrates. If commercialization becomes likely, a broad range of environmental risks will need to be assessed based on our growing knowledge of methane hydrates as well as, for example, the impacts of offshore oil and gas drilling (including on the seafloor and submarine slopes), and leaks during natural gas production and transport.

Read more about methane hydrates in the UNEP Year Book 2008.

Recent observations and knowledge

Scientists are interested in quantifying the amount of methane being released from all emission sources in the rapidly warming Arctic. They also want to better understand the effects that climate change has on these releases. However, they strongly disagree about whether global warming could conceivably trigger – in the foreseeable future – catastrophic atmospheric releases of methane from destabilized methane hydrates in this region.

As global warming continues, methane releases to the atmosphere related to thawing Arctic permafrost (but not to the methane hydrates beneath the permafrost) are expected to continue. A recent study shows that methane emissions from the East Siberian Arctic Shelf are more than twice what were previously believed. The authors suggest that these emissions result from the degradation of submarine permafrost over thousands of years. This appears to be a source of methane emissions to the atmosphere at least as significant as Arctic tundra, which is considered a major source of methane emissions.

Unexpected levels of methane have also been discovered coming from cracks in Arctic sea ice and areas where there is partial sea ice. Further research is needed to determine where this methane comes from. The enhanced methane from these cracks could be produced by a form of ocean ventilation, whereby the ocean interacts with the air and methane escapes into the atmosphere.

It is not only in the Arctic that scientists are finding out more about methane emissions and methane hydrates. According to a recent study of the **Antarctic ice sheet**, pressure and temperature conditions favour methane hydrate formation down to sediment depths of about 300 metres in West Antarctica and 700 metres in East Antarctica. The authors have calculated that the sub-Antarctic hydrate inventory could be of the same order of magnitude as that of recent estimates made for Arctic permafrost. They do not suggest, however, that these methane hydrates could be a source of atmospheric methane emissions.

The Antarctic ice sheet

The Antarctic ice sheet is the Earth's largest single mass of ice, extending over almost 14 million km² and containing over 90% of the freshwater in the form of ice on the planet. In East Antarctica the ice sheet rests on a major land mass, while in West Antarctica the bed can extend to more than 2500 metres below sea level. It was recently reported that a large section of the West Antarctic ice sheet is melting into the sea.

© USGS Gas Hydrates Lab

Searching for answers to some complex questions

Scientific and technological advances are being made in a number of countries, with the aim of exploring the possibilities of producing natural gas from methane hydrates. In March 2013 the world's first offshore methane hydrate production test was conducted off the coast of Honshu Island, Japan. The test site was chosen based on seismic and well data indicating methane hydrate-rich sedimentary layers in this area. About 120,000 m^3 of methane gas was produced from the hydrate-bearing sediments.

Scientists and engineers are analyzing the data collected. At the same time, an international team of researchers has been studying sediment samples containing gas hydrates obtained from layers beneath the deep seafloor in the Nankai Trough off Japan. Highly sophisticated techniques were required to retrieve these samples and keep them at their natural, stable conditions.

Japan and other countries are assessing the extent of available methane hydrate deposits while simultaneously looking at technologies for commercially viable natural gas production. In Japan a long-term production test (e.g. one lasting over 18 months) now needs to be carried out to prove that sustained methane production from gas hydrates is viable. This is the critical research and development step on the path to eventual commercialization. Japan has announced plans to make its extraction technology commercially viable by the end of this decade.

In the early 2000s a team of Canadian and Japanese scientists succeeded in extracting methane from the Mallik gas hydrate site by heating the reservoir. Still better results were obtained in 2008 by lowering the reservoir's pressure without resorting to heating. After the experiment ended, technicians on-site expressed confidence that production could have continued even longer. The success of this second land-based experiment indicates that decompression techniques may be a more viable route to commercialization of methane hydrates.

With the necessary technology and favourable market conditions, natural gas production based on extraction of methane from methane hydrates may become economically viable in some regions and for some reservoirs. Nevertheless, complex questions remain to be answered – not only about how to achieve this, but also about the future environmental impacts of continuing to use natural gas as a fuel.

It is widely recognized that international cooperative efforts are necessary to address environmental issues, including the links between fossil fuel combustion and climate change. Such cooperative efforts are carried out by the *Global Methane Initiative* and the Global Carbon Project, which produces regularly updated calculations of the global methane budget and trends. The most comprehensive global methane inventory can be found in the Emissions Database for Global Atmospheric Research (EDGAR).

The Global Methane Initiative

Countries and organizations cooperating in the Global Methane Initiative (GMI) aim to build capacity and overcome barriers to methane reduction projects around the world. The GMI database contains information about these projects and many other activities.

Estimated global anthropogenic methane emissions by source, 2010

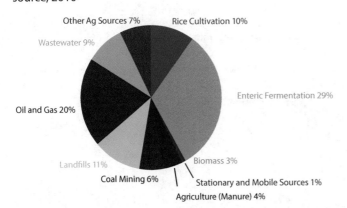

Other Ag Sources 7%
Rice Cultivation 10%
Wastewater 9%
Enteric Fermentation 29%
Oil and Gas 20%
Landfills 11%
Biomass 3%
Coal Mining 6%
Stationary and Mobile Sources 1%
Agriculture (Manure) 4%

© Global Methane Initiative

Addressing big questions and continuing international cooperation

Methane hydrates represent a potentially large source of natural gas, although we do not know the size of the global methane hydrate inventory. Lessons being learned in countries today about oil and gas drilling, including the extraction of **unconventional natural gas**, may be relevant to the development of future methane hydrate policies.

Unconventional natural gas

Sources of unconventional natural gas include shale gas (found in shale deposits), coal bed methane (extracted from coal beds) and tight gas (trapped underground in impermeable rock formations). As of 2012, these types of unconventional gas had reached an estimated 18% of global natural gas production. Shale gas output is concentrated in the United States, but is rapidly spreading to other parts of the world.

© LINN Energy

© JOGMEC

Research in recent decades, aimed at resolving some of the uncertainty about methane hydrates as a potential energy source, has involved international and interdisciplinary cooperation and wide information sharing. It has also benefited from work in which the public and private sectors are both engaged. Important questions that need to be addressed through such efforts include:

- What can scientists tell us about potential releases of methane to the ocean-atmosphere system due to the breakdown of methane hydrates?
- How likely does production of methane from hydrates appear to be? What is a reasonable timeline for commercialization, and what factors might affect this timeline?
- What is the relationship between methane hydrates (and eventual offshore drilling to extract them) and seafloor destabilization?
- What would the environmental, economic and social impacts of methane hydrates-based natural gas production be?

Further information about methane hydrates

Beaudoin, Y.C., et al. (eds.) (in press). Frozen Heat: Global Outlook on Methane Gas Hydrates, Vol. 2

Cyranoski, D. (2013). Japanese test coaxes fire from ice. First attempt to extract methane from frozen hydrates far beneath the ocean shows promise Nature, 23 April http://www.nature.com/news/japanese-test-coaxes-fire-from-ice-1.12858

Kort, E.A., et al. (2012). Atmospheric observations of Arctic Ocean methane emissions up to 82° north. Nature Geoscience, 5:318-321 http://www.nature.com/ngeo/journal/v5/n5/full/ngeo1452.html#access

National Research Council (2010). Realizing the Energy Potential of Methane Hydrate for the United States http://www.nap.edu/catalog.php?record_id=12831

Revkin, A. (2013). Arctic Methane Credibility Bomb. New York Times, 25 July. http://dotearth.blogs.nytimes.com/2013/07/25/arctic-methane-credibility-bomb/

Ruppel, C.D. (2011a). Methane Hydrates and Contemporary Climate Change. Nature Education Knowledge, 3, 10, 29 http://www.nature.com/scitable/knowledge/library/methane-hydrates-and-contemporary-climate-change-24314790

Ruppel, C. (2011b). MITEI Natural Gas Report, Supplementary Paper on Methane Hydrates. Methane Hydrates and the Future of Natural Gas. Supplement to MIT (Massachusetts Institute of Technology). In The Future of Natural Gas. An Interdisciplinary MIT Study https://mitei.mit.edu/system/files/Supplementary_Paper_SP_2_4_Hydrates.pdf

Shakhova, N., et al. (2014). Ebullition and storm-induced methane release from the East Siberian Arctic Shelf. Nature Geoscience, 7, 64-70 http://www.nature.com/ngeo/journal/v7/n1/full/ngeo2007.html

University of California at Irvine (2013). W.M. Keck Foundation grants UCI $1 million for deep-ocean power science lab. News release, 18 January http://news.uci.edu/press-releases/w-m-keck-foundation-grants-uci-1-million-for-deep-ocean-power-science-lab/

USGS (United States Geological Survey) (2013). Groundbreaking Gas Hydrate Research. News release, 13 February. http://www.usgs.gov/blogs/features/usgs_top_story/groundbreaking-gas-hydrate-research//

USGS (no date). The U.S. Geological Survey Gas Hydrates Project. Submarine Slope Destabilization http://woodshole.er.usgs.gov/project-pages/hydrates/seafloor.html

Wadham, J.L., et al. (2012). Potential methane reservoirs beneath Antarctica. Nature, 488, 633-637 http://www.nature.com/nature/journal/v488/n7413/full/nature11374.html

World Oceans Review (2014). WOR 3. Marine Resources – Opportunities and Risks http://worldoceanreview.com/wp-content/downloads/wor3/WOR3_english.pdf

UNEP Year Book 2014 emerging issues update

Realizing the Potential of Citizen Science

Getting involved: citizen science

Since prehistoric times people have observed and recorded the natural world in order to survive. However, curiosity about the world around us, and the pleasure we take in it, are other reasons we pay careful attention to and make records of flora and fauna, water bodies, the weather and other phenomena. In China locust outbreaks have been tracked for thousands of years; in Japan the flowering of cherry trees has been marked for 1200 years. Successful agricultural harvests have always depended on knowing what to plant where, and how to make crops grow well.

Today people's inborn curiosity is increasingly being harnessed by science. Volunteers are collecting and/or analyzing data, as well as contributing to scientific studies in different ways. This is called *citizen science*. Simply put, this means public participation in scientific research. Citizen science can help researchers obtain a wide perspective and deep data. It helps answer complex questions about, for example, air pollution, biodiversity conservation, urbanization patterns, and changes in agricultural production and fisheries worldwide. Taking part in citizen science activities also raises awareness, increases local interest, and contributes to more informed policy decisions.

What is citizen science?

In citizen science people who are not professional scientists take part in one or more aspects of science— systematic collection and analysis of data, development of technology, testing of natural phenomena and dissemination of the results of activities. They mainly participate on a voluntary basis.

Volunteers taking part in environment-related studies can sample wide geographic areas more quickly and at lower cost than professional research teams. Projects that involve 'birders' are among the largest and oldest citizen science initiatives. The Audubon Society's Christmas Bird Count began in North America in 1900. The Audubon Society reports that 'from feeder-watchers and field observers to count compilers and regional editors, everyone who takes part in the Christmas Bird Count does it for love of birds and the excitement of friendly

© techNyou

For video links please go to http://www.youtube.com/watch?v=N6eN3Pll4U8

competition – and with the knowledge that their efforts are making a difference for science and bird conservation.'

The Big Garden Bird Watch in the United Kingdom is also one of the world's largest citizen science activities, with over 400,000 people taking part at 228 locations. The Audubon Society's international Great Backyard Bird Count has been conducted since 1998. The first global version of the Great Backyard Bird Count took place in 2013. These projects demonstrate three of the main advantages of citizen science: large numbers of participants are able to provide enormous amounts of data, from far-reaching locations, and data collection may take place over long periods.

© Gill Conquest/ ExCiteS, University of London

Trends and recent developments in citizen science

Citizen science can go beyond simple data collection to help shape fundamental questions about our world and provide intriguing answers. Participation has grown partly due to the Internet, social media, and other new and increasingly affordable technologies. Once the public was mainly involved in activities concerned with, for example, the environment and astronomy. Today opportunities to volunteer to take part in scientific research have exploded into many disciplines, from analyzing cancer data to tracking genetic mysteries to theoretical physics.

Scientists are increasingly recognizing the benefits of public knowledge and open participation. The statistical power provided by large amounts of data can be used to obtain valuable insights into scientific questions. For example, gamers taking part in FoldIt, an online game whose purpose is to decipher how proteins fold, figured out the structure of an enzyme involved with HIV within three weeks of being given the problem.

Data and other information generated through citizen science projects have been shown to be reliable and accurate. High-quality data generated from these projects are reinforced through appropriate research protocols, proper training and oversight measures, as well as the application and utilization of new statistical and high-performance computing tools that eliminate sample bias and remove measurement errors or spatial clustering. There is evidence that data from citizen science research projects are increasingly accepted in the academic literature.

Not only does citizen science contribute to scientific knowledge, but the experience generated through public participation provides the benefits of better access to information and motivation of local communities.

Technologies contributing to the growth of citizen science include satellites, which provide a wealth of data in need of analysis (possibilities to analyze large data sets are available to citizen scientists), global positioning systems (GPS) and

Social demand and data collectors

Data are being collected by citizen scientists worldwide. This includes collection of data on radiation following the Fukushima nuclear accident in 2011, to projects like MammalMAP (which aims to put all visual evidence of mammals in Africa into an open access database to help conservation planning), to using cameras attached to kites and balloons to measure and monitor oil spills' impact on the environment.

smartphone apps, which are widely used today throughout the world. Volunteers can become *data collectors and users* even in remote locations.

Citizen science faces a number of challenges in terms of both coordination and organization, but potential solutions exist. These include: the use of innovative information and communication technology, such as online searchable database modularization; well-defined and structured project leadership; and mechanisms to sustain people's interest in participation, as well as to respond to the range of individuals' motives for participating, such as intellectual challenges, direct livelihood benefits, or the opportunity to take part in updating traditional knowledge.

© Jerome Lewis/ ExCiteS, University of London

Renewing and understanding traditional knowledge

As participation grows, citizen science is having an impact in some far-flung parts of the world. It is not only a valuable hobby for people in developed countries who enjoy helping to acquire new knowledge. It is also a concept of science that serves people. Several research projects have involved working with indigenous people on topics relevant to their environments, livelihoods and cultures. Through these projects, people have a greater voice in the management of their resources.

In Finland major restoration of a river and its catchment areas has been taken place in the Southern Boreal region of North Karelia. Local fishermen (together with *Snowchange*) have led restoration activities on the heavily damaged Jukajoki River. Local people, using a collaborative management approach as well as traditional knowledge and supporting scientific measures, have identified damaged sites in the catchment areas and taken a number of steps to improve water protection. The successful Jukajoki River initiative shows how citizen science and traditional knowledge can be applied in community-based ecosystem restoration.

Snowchange Cooperative

The Snowchange Cooperative, which began in Finland in 2000, has worked for a decade and a half with both indigenous and local traditional societies to advance their traditions and foster a dialogue with science.

In the Congo Basin, researchers, artists and information and communication technology (ICT) specialists have come together with the Bayaka pygmies to help them map and patrol their forests. The forest inhabitants use handheld devices to map and protect sacred and valuable trees, and to document logging activities. They have been enabled to monitor the forests in such a way that the data collected have been used as evidence to help negotiate with logging companies.

Cybertracker is an innovative software program that can be used by people who neither read nor write. On a rugged handheld computer a touch screen displays a menu of pictograms linked to a GPS system, allowing observations

that are made in the field to be instantly and accurately recorded. By using Cybertracker, the San people living in the Kalahari contribute their knowledge of animal behaviour and tracking to environmental monitoring projects. Wildlife conservation efforts are being strengthened thanks to this traditional expertise. In Northern Australia, indigenous women rangers in remote areas also use Cybertracker to record information about water quality, movement of animals, fire management, and the presence and density of weeds. Over 700 independent projects in 75 countries have used the Cybertracker.

Activities such as these illustrate how various social and traditional groups can make major contributions through citizen science, and how this community approach can help put vulnerable groups on a more equal footing with other environmental stakeholders while helping to protect their resources and ultimately influencing the governance structure with respect to both their natural resources and the environment.

As technological advances are made, enabling more people to take part in the exploration of our world, one opportunity presented by citizen science is the growing capacity to involve communities and strengthen civil society while protecting the environment.

Improving coordination to achieve greater impacts

One of the recognized benefits of citizen science is that it brings people together, either directly or through social networking – including local communities, administrative authorities and policy-makers. When applied to local natural resources management, for example, it can lead to solutions and decision-making processes that consider the viewpoints of all those concerned.

The current and potential role of citizen science is increasingly recognized regionally and internationally. For example, the European Commission's Green Paper on Citizen Science recognizes the value of the participatory science approach and its relevance to EU strategy. Practitioners worldwide participate in coordination and policy platforms, such as the Citizen Science Association and the European Citizen Science Association. Establishing such communities of practices aims to promote collaboration and knowledge sharing.

© Citizen Cyberlab

For video links please go to http://www.youtube.com/watch?v=HQtfrMs-hl4&list=U UhsdtAyejxQmiZ6RjxtYTAw

© Gill Conquest / ExCiteS, University of London

Barriers to realizing the full potential of citizen science nevertheless exist. Approaches to overcoming them include:

- Better coordination among scientists, project developers and others to make use of (and collaborate with) relevant already established and proven citizen science projects; this could reduce project redundancy, which can confuse the public and appear to constitute 're-inventing the wheel'
- Stronger recognition by scientific communities of the value of data generated by citizen science) - especially in peer-reviewed processes – so that information and knowledge generated from citizen science projects can gain better appreciation and inspire more confidence
- Coordination internationally to better aggregate and analyze data generated by citizen science, which could help reveal valuable data sets useful to scientists, policy-makers and others

Further information about citizen science

European Commission (EC) (2013). Green Paper on Citizen Science http://www.societize.eu/sites/default/files/Green%20Paper%20on%20Citizen%20Science%202013.pdf

Bonney, R. et al. (2014). Next steps for citizen science. Science, 343 http://ccrec.ucsc.edu/sites/default/files/Bonney%20et%20al%202014%20Science%20v.343-p.1436-7.pdf

Conrad, C.C. and Hilchey, K.G. (2011). A review of citizen science and community-based environmental monitoring: issues and opportunities. Environment Monitoring Assessment, 176(1-4):273-91 http://link.springer.com/article/10.1007%2Fs10661-010-1582-5

Coren, M.J. and Fast Company. (2011, September 20). Foldit gamers solve riddle of HIV enzyme within 3 weeks. Scientific American. Retrieved June 9, 2014. http://www.scientificamerican.com/article/foldit-gamers-solve-riddle/

Danielsen, F. et al. (2014). A multicountry assessment of tropical resource monitoring by local communities. BioScience, Vol. 64 No. 3 http://bioscience.oxfordjournals.org/content/early/2014/02/18/biosci.biu001.abstract

Dickinson, J. L. et al. (2010). Citizen science as an ecological research tool: Challenges and benefits. Annual Review of Ecology, Evolution, and, 41:149–72 http://www.annualreviews.org/doi/abs/10.1146/annurev-ecolsys-102209-144636?journalCode=ecolsys

Dickinson, J. L. et al. (2012). Citizen Science: Public Participation in Environmental Research. Comstock Publishing Associates http://www.cornellpress.cornell.edu/book/?GCOI=80140100107290

Franzoni, C. and Sauermann, H. (2014). Crowd science: The organization of scientific research in open collaborative projects. Research Policy, 43: 1-20 http://scistarter.com/blog/wp-content/uploads/2013/04/SSRN-id2167538211.pdf

Miller-Rushing, A. et al. (2012). The history of public participation in ecological research. Frontiers in Ecology and the Environment, 285 http://www.esajournals.org/doi/abs/10.1890/110278

Mustonen, T. (2014). Power discourses of firsh death: Case of Linnunsuo peat production. Ambio. 43(2):234-243. March 2014 http://link.springer.com/article/10.1007/s13280-013-0425-3

Mustonen, T. (2013). Oral histories as a baseline of landscape restoration – co-management and watershed knowledge in Jukajoki river. Fennia international journal of geography. 191(2) http://ojs.tsv.fi/index.php/fennia/article/view/7637

Openscientist. (2011). Finalizing a definition of "Citizen Science" and "Citizen Scientists". Retrieved from http://www.openscientist.org/2011/09/finalizing-definition-of-citizen.html

Rowland, K. (2012). Citizen science goes 'Extreme'. Nature. February 2012 doi:10.1038/nature.2012.10054 http://www.nature.com/news/citizen-science-goes-extreme-1.10054

Sullivan, B. L. et al. (2014). The eBird enterprise: An integrated approach to development and application of citizen science. Biological Conservation, 169: 31–40. http://www.sciencedirect.com/science/article/pii/S0006320713003820

UNEP Year Book 2014 emerging issues update

Air Pollution: World's Worst Environmental Health Risk

Unacceptable environmental, social and economic costs

There is an urgent need to reduce levels of air pollution globally. Although air quality measures have had positive results at some locations in the world, millions of people in both developing and developed countries die prematurely every year because of long-term exposure to air pollutants. The health of many more is seriously affected.

Most cities where outdoor air pollution is monitored do not meet the World Health Organization (WHO) guidelines for acceptable pollutant levels. People who live in these cities have increased risks of stroke, heart disease, lung cancer, chronic and acute respiratory diseases (including asthma) and other health problems. Indoor air pollution is another major cause of poor health and premature death, especially in developing countries.

Sources of air pollution include traffic (especially diesel vehicles), industrial sectors (from brick making to oil and gas production), power plants, cooking and heating with solid fuels (e.g. coal, wood, crop waste), forest fires and open burning of municipal waste and agricultural residues.

Particulate matter 2.5 micrometres or less in diameter ($PM_{2.5}$) is produced by incomplete combustion of fossil fuels and biomass and one of the biggest concerns. One-hundredth the thickness of a human hair, $PM_{2.5}$ can penetrate deep into the lungs and blood stream and is dangerous at any concentration. The International Agency for Research on Cancer (IARC) concluded in 2013 that particulate matter is carcinogenic to humans. Ground-level ozone (O_3) is another important air pollutant, which damages human health and crops. It is estimated that global losses to soybean, maize and wheat crops due to ground-level ozone pollution could be US$17-35 billion per year by 2030. Reducing emissions of $PM_{2.5}$ and ground-level ozone not only has an immediate effect on air quality, but also mitigates near-term climate change and helps achieve food security.

Over 3.5 million people die each year from outdoor air pollution. Between 2005 and 2010, the death rate rose by 4%

worldwide, by 5% in China and by 12% in India. *Cost of air pollution* to society in 2010 was estimated at US$1.4 trillion in China and US$0.5 trillion in India according to a recent study by the Organisation for Economic Co-Operation and Development (OECD). In Europe, exposure to air pollution from road transport costs about US$137 billion per year and harm caused by air pollution from the 10,000 largest polluting facilities in 2009 – including through lost lives, poor health and crop damage – was about US$140-230 billion.

The economic cost of air pollution

The cost of air pollution to the world's most advanced economies plus India and China is estimated to be US$3.5 trillion per year in lives lost and ill health. In OECD countries the monetary impact of death and illness due to outdoor air pollution in 2010 is estimated to have been US$1.7 trillion.

Improving air quality has the potential to provide enormous economic benefits. In the United States, the direct economic benefits of reducing $PM_{2.5}$ and ground-level ozone pollution under the 1990 Clean Air Act Amendments are estimated to be up to 90 times the cost of implementing them. About 85% of the economic benefits would be due to fewer premature deaths linked to reducing $PM_{2.5}$ in the outdoor environment, with the early deaths of 230,000 people avoided in the year 2020 alone.

Read more about air pollution in the UNEP Year Book 2010 sections on harmful substances and climate change.

Air pollution: the leading cause of environmentally related deaths

The health impacts of air pollution are much larger than was thought only a few years ago. The World Health Organization (WHO) estimates that in 2012 around 7 million premature deaths resulted from air pollution, more than double previous estimates. The new estimate is based on increasing knowledge of air pollution-related diseases and use of improved air quality measurements and technology. According to WHO, outdoor air pollution caused 3.7 million premature deaths in 2012. Indoor air pollution is responsible for about 4.3 million premature deaths every year.

Outdoor air quality is rapidly deteriorating in major cities in low and middle income countries (LMICs). The WHO guideline for average annual particulate matter (PM_{10}) levels is 20 micrograms per cubic metre. For fine particles ($PM_{2.5}$) the average annual level is 10 micrograms per cubic metre and 25 micrograms per cubic metre for a 24 hour period. Air pollution levels in cities in LMICs sometimes far exceed these levels. In Kathmandu, Nepal, for example, $PM_{2.5}$ levels of over 500 micrograms per cubic metre have been measured.

About 3 billion people in the world cook and heat their homes with coal and biomass. Air pollutant emissions need to be reduced not only from these inefficient energy systems, but also from agricultural waste incineration, forest fires and charcoal production. In Africa, due to the rapid growth of its cities and megacities, a large increase in air pollutant emissions from burning of fossil fuels and traditional biomass use for energy services is expected in the near future. They

could contribute 50% of global emissions in 2030, according to some estimates. A World Bank study found that in Sub-Saharan Africa implementation of low-sulphur fuels (50 ppm) and cleaning up of vehicles, including motorcycles, would result in health benefits estimated at US$43 billion over a ten-year period.

Effective policies and strategies to reduce air pollution work. In many countries, emissions and concentrations of harmful pollutants such as carbon monoxide (CO), sulphur dioxide (SO_2) and lead are lower than a few decades ago. Africa has made good progress in introducing cleaner fuels with the phase-out of leaded petrol. Swiss studies confirm the substantial health benefits of air quality improvements, even in a country with relatively low levels of air pollution.

Many efforts to reduce air pollution go hand in hand with technological enhancements that also improve energy efficiency, thereby producing additional economic and environmental benefits. Although technology is available to make vehicles, agriculture, industrial installations, power plants, waste treatment facilities and other sources less polluting, innovations and their adoption may take time. Moreover, progress in emission reductions per unit can often be outweighed by rapid increases in the number of units (e.g. vehicles).

Air pollution in developed countries has decreased in recent years, partly due to tighter emission controls, including on vehicles. Nevertheless, evidence suggests that road transport accounted for 50% of the cost of the health impacts of air pollution – both death and illness – in OECD countries in 2010 (or close to US$1 trillion). With the rapid growth of traffic in developing countries such as China and India, air pollution has outpaced the adoption of tighter vehicle emission standards. There is insufficient evidence to estimate the share of road transport in total health impacts due to air pollution in developing countries.

Choking to death

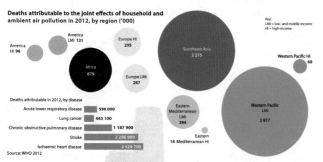

Deaths attributable to the joint effects of household and ambient air pollution in 2012, by region ('000)

Key:
LMI = low- and middle income
HI = high-income

America HI 96
America LMI 131
Europe HI 295
Europe LMI 287
Africa 679
Southeast Asia 2 275
Western Pacific HI 68
Eastern Mediterranean LMI 394
Eastern Mediterranean HI 14
Western Pacific LMI 2 817

Deaths attributable in 2012, by disease

Disease	
Acute lower respiratory disease	596 000
Lung cancer	443 100
Chronic obstructive pulmonary disease	1 187 900
Stroke	2 296 900
Ischaemic heart disease	2 529 700

Source: WHO 2012

The transboundary challenge of air pollution

Investing in implementing effective policies to make air cleaner will cost countries far less in the long run than allowing air pollution to worsen. Air pollution is a transboundary issue, and lessons can be learned from past successes in any country. In many cases technological improvements to reduce air pollution can pay for themselves as additional benefits such as energy efficiency are realized.

Enforcement of existing regulations is essential. As part of China's campaign to tackle air pollution, fines for polluting in the first three months of 2014 were ten times the total in the same period the previous year, and more than three times as many polluting companies were fined. The government has announced plans to take up to 6 million vehicles that do not meet emission standards off the roads by the end of 2014. A cap was placed on new vehicle sales in 2013.

The Global Fuel Economy Initiative is working to improve the fuel economy capacity of the global vehicle fleet. Successful international cooperation to phase out leaded petrol under the UNEP-led Partnership for Clean Fuel and Vehicles (PCFV) – and more recent actions to reduce $PM_{2.5}$ emissions and promote a shift to low-sulphur fuels – suggest that the global fleet is becoming less polluting. When the PCFV was launched in 2002, approximately half the world's countries used leaded petrol. As of October 2013, only six countries were still using a small amount. The PCFV phase-out avoids an estimated 1.3 million premature deaths per year.

Research is being carried out in a number of countries to reduce emissions of air pollutants from cookstoves. Over the years, many types of improved cooking stoves have been developed. For example, the Ruiru Youth Community Empowerment Program in Kenya has developed a less polluting firewood-burning stove that is up to 60% more efficient than the open fires traditionally used in rural areas. Youth volunteers have trained around 16,000 local women on the advantages of the new stoves and how to install them. A household cooking and heating stoves initiative of the Climate and Clean Air Coalition (CCAC) helps develop

Annual Average PM 10 Levels of Major Cities

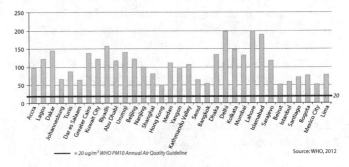

— = 20 ug/m³ WHO PM10 Annual Air Quality Guideline   Source: WHO, 2012

test protocols and standards to ensure lower emissions from such stoves. It also supports projects that scale up alternative cooking solutions.

In several countries low-cost monitoring devices are being developed to measure air pollution levels and exposures. Smartphone apps, for example, allow users to check air quality and look at real-time data on major outdoor air pollution. Also under development are online platforms for releases of real-time monitoring information. UNEP's Surya project uses mobile phones to monitor indoor air pollution.

© Safia Osman

Meeting agreed standards to achieve economic and health benefits

Countries are curbing air pollution by enforcing air quality standards and stimulating the development of cleaner technologies. Target-setting to improve air quality should be based on the latest science – including the best possible estimates of impacts of air pollution on the health of people and ecosystems. Scientists and policy-makers worldwide have ready access to *internationally agreed guidelines* such as the World Health Organization (WHO) air quality guidelines, the Environmental Health Criteria documents and International Agency for Research on Cancer (IARC) studies.

International air quality guidelines

The WHO air quality guidelines provide assessments of the health effects of air pollution and thresholds for pollution levels that are harmful to health. They inform policy makers and provide appropriate targets for a broad range of air quality management policy options in different parts of the world. Environmental Health Criteria documents address the effects of chemicals or combinations of chemicals and physical and biological agents on human health and the environment. The work of the IARC is focused on cancer.

Some countries are more advanced than others in regard to establishing limit and target values as well as requirements to reduce emissions from pollutant sources, monitor emissions and concentrations, and determine exposures. Countries lacking experience can profit from the knowledge already acquired by more advanced ones, keeping in mind local and regional differences including climatic conditions, income levels and consumption patterns.

It has long been recognized that air pollutants are easily transported across borders. Over 50 countries are engaged in effective cooperative work under the United Nations Economic Commission for Europe (UNECE) Convention on Long-range Transboundary Air Pollution. Existing cooperation

between government agencies and other bodies at national and regional levels through networks and other mechanisms can be further expanded. Air quality assessments would help identify gaps in countries' capacity to address air pollution and identify new opportunities for cooperation.

Data collection and sharing is of fundamental importance in addressing air quality issues and measuring policy effectiveness. Despite some progress, air quality data are often scattered or incomplete and not easily available.

Emissions of outdoor air pollution from major sources can be reduced through policies and investments that support less polluting and more energy-efficient transport, housing and industries, as well as improved power generation, municipal waste management and agricultural practices. Actions that reduce air pollution can also reduce climate impacts. Black carbon, for example, is one of three short-lived climate pollutants targeted for reduction by the CCAC along with methane (CH_4) and hydrofluorocarbons (HFCs). It has been estimated that 'fast action' on black carbon and methane would potentially cut the rate of climate change in half for the next several decades, as well as reducing air pollution-related deaths by as much as 2.4 million per year and avoiding annual crop losses of 50 to more than 100 million tonnes. Opportunities clearly exist to tackle air pollution and other severe health and environmental problems cost-effectively using integrated approaches.

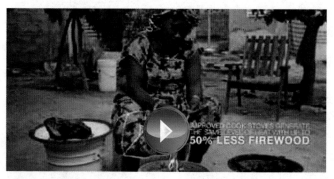

© UNEP

For video links please go to http://vimeo.com/80295930

Further information about air pollution

Avnery, S. et al. (2011). Global crop yield reductions due to surface ozone exposure: 2. Year 2030 potential crop production losses and economic damage under two scenarios of O3 pollution. Atmospheric Environment, 45, 13, 2297-2309 http://www.sciencedirect.com/science/article/pii/S1352231011000070

Bell, M.L. and Davis, D.L. (2001). Reassessment of the lethal London fog of 1952: novel indicators of acute and chronic consequences of acute exposure to air pollution. Environmental Health Perspectives, Suppl. 3, 389-394 http://www.ncbi.nlm.nih.gov/pubmed/11427388

Burnett, R.T., et al. (2014). An Integrated Risk Function for Estimating the Global Burden of Disease Attributable to Ambient Fine Particulate Matter Exposure. Environmental Health Perspectives, DOI:10.1289/ehp.1307049 http://ehp.niehs.nih.gov/1307049/

Duggan, J. (2014). China to scrap millions of cars to ease pollution. China to take 6 million old cars off the road in a bid to improve air quality in smog-hit regions. News article, 27 May http://www.theguardian.com/environment/chinas-choice/2014/may/27/china-scrap-millions-cars-reduce-air-pollution

e-360 (2013). Beijing to limit new cars by 40 percent in anti-pollution drive. News article, 5 November http://e360.yale.edu/digest/beijing_to_limit_new_cars__by_40_percent_in_anti-pollution_drive/3994/

EEA (European Environment Agency) (2011). Industrial air pollution cost Europe up to € 169 billion in 2009, EEA reveals http://www.eea.europa.eu/media/newsreleases/industrial-air-pollution-cost-europe

EEA (2013a). Reducing the € 45 billion health cost of air pollution from lorries http://www.eea.europa.eu/media/newsreleases/reducing-the-20ac-45-billion

EEA (2013b). New Sensing Technologies and Methods for Air-Pollution Monitoring http://www.cost.eunetair.it/cost/meetings/docCopen/11-BOOKLET_TD1105_EEA_Copenhagen.pdf

Evans, J., et al. (2013). Estimates of global mortality attributable to particulate air pollution using satellite imagery. Environmental Research, 120, 20,33-42 http://patarnott.com/satsens/pdf/globalMortalityPM_satellite.pdf

Fang, Yuanyuan et al. (2013). Impacts of 21st century climate change on global air pollution-related premature mortality. Climatic Change, 121(2):239-253 http://link.springer.com/article/10.1007%2Fs10584-013-0847-8

Gurung, A. and Bell, M.L. (2012). Exposure to airborne particulate matter in Kathmandu Valley, Nepal. Journal of Exposure Science and Environmental Epidemiology, 22(3):235-242

IARC (International Agency for Research on Cancer) (2013). Air Pollution and Cancer. IARC Scientific Publication No. 161 (K. Straif, A. Cohen and J. Samet, eds.) http://www.iarc.fr/en/publications/books/sp161/index.php

IARC and WHO (World Health Organization) (2013). IARC: Outdoor air pollution a leading environmental cause of cancer deaths. News release, 17 October http://www.iarc.fr/en/media-centre/pr/2013/pdfs/pr221_E.pdf

Liousse, C., et al. (2014). Explosive growth in African combustion emissions from 2005 to 2030. Environmental Research Letters, 9, 3, 035003 http://iopscience.iop.org/1748-9326/9/3/035003/article

Loomis, D., et al. (2014). The International Agency for Research on Cancer (IARC) evaluation of the carcinogenicity of outdoor air pollution: focus on China. Chin J Cancer. 33(4):189-96 http://www.ncbi.nlm.nih.gov/pubmed/24694836

OECD (Organization for Economic Co-operation and Development) (2012). OECD Environmental Outlook to 2050 (Chapter 6, "Health and Environment") http://www.oecd.org/environment/indicators-modelling-outlooks/oecdenvironmentaloutlookto2050theconsequencesofinaction.htm

OECD (2014). The cost of air pollution: Health impacts of road transport http://www.oecd.org/environment/cost-of-air-pollution.htm

Pyper, J. (2014). Air pollution is a $1.7T health problem, OECD finds. News story, 22 May http://www.eenews.net/stories/1060000041

UNEP (United Nations Environment Programme) (2010). "Harmful Substances and Hazardous Wastes" and "Climate Change" chapters in UNEP Year Book 2010: New Science and Developments in Our Changing Environment http://www.unep.org/yearbook/2010/PDF/2_Harmful_substances_2010_low.pdf http://www.unep.org/yearbook/2010/PDF/3_climate_change_2010_low.pdf

UNEP (2011) Near-term Climate Protection and Clean Air Benefits: Actions for Controlling Short-Lived Climate Forcers - A UNEP Synthesis Report http://www.unep.org/ccac/Publications/Publications/tabid/130293/Default.aspx#sthash.89chc6YI.dpuf

University of Massachusetts (2014). Updating Air Pollution Measurement Methods with UMass Amherst Air Quality, Health Effects. News release, 6 January http://www.umass.edu/newsoffice/article/updating-air-pollution-measurement-methods

US EPA (United States Environmental Protection Agency) (2011). Second Prospective Study – 1990 to 2020 http://www.epa.gov/cleanairactbenefits/prospective2-2.html

US EPA (2013a). EPA Village Green Project http://village-green.epa.gov

US EPA (2013b). Scientists evaluate air sensors developed during EPA's Air Sensor Evaluation and Collaboration Event http://www.epa.gov/nerl/features/sensors.html

US EPA (2013c). Next generation air monitoring http://www.epa.gov/research/airscience/air-sensor-research.htm

US EPA (2014). Clean Cookstove Research: http://www.epa.gov/research/airscience/air-cleancookstove.htm

Wang Hongyi (2014). University unveils new air purifier technology. News article, 7 January. http://www.chinadaily.com.cn/china/2014-01/07/content_17219181.htm

WHO (World Health Organization) (2005). WHO air quality guidelines for particulate matter, ozone, nitrogen dioxide and sulfur dioxide. Global update 2005. Summary of risk assessment http://whqlibdoc.who.int/hq/2006/WHO_SDE_PHE_OEH_06.02_eng.pdf?ua=1

WHO (2014a). Air quality deteriorating in many of the world's cities. News release, 7 May http://www.who.int/mediacentre/news/releases/2014/air-quality/en/

WHO (2014b). 7 million premature deaths annually linked to air pollution. New release, 25 March http://www.who.int/mediacentre/news/releases/2014/air-pollution/en/

WHO (2014c). Ambient (outdoor) air quality and health. Fact Sheet No. 313, update March 2014 http://www.who.int/mediacentre/factsheets/fs313/en/

WHO (2014d). Frequently Asked Questions. Ambient and Household Air Pollution and Health. Update 2014 http://www.who.int/phe/health_topics/outdoorair/databases/faqs_air_pollution.pdf?ua=1

World Bank (2013). An analysis of physical and monetary losses of environmental health and natural resources. Vol. 1 of India - Diagnostic assessment of select environmental challenges http://documents.worldbank.org/curated/en/2013/06/18009327/india-diagnostic-assessment-select-environmental-challenges-vol-1-3-analysis-physical-monetary-losses-environmental-health-natural-resources

World Bank and the Development Research Center of the State Council, the People's Republic of China (2014). Urban China: Toward Efficient, Inclusive, and Sustainable Urbanization http://www.worldbank.org/content/dam/Worldbank/document/EAP/China/WEB-Urban-China.pdf

UNEP Year Book 2014 emerging issues update

Plastic Debris in the Ocean

Continous flows of plastic to the marine environment

Every year large amounts of plastic debris enter the ocean from both land- and sea-based activities, such as fisheries and tourism, and poor waste management. While the total amount in the ocean is unknown, plastic is found all over the world including in the polar regions, far from its source.

Floating plastic can be transported great distances by ocean currents. Although plastic debris is most commonly observed on shorelines, it also accumulates in mid-ocean *'gyres'*, natural circulation features that tend to trap floating material. Some of the material sinks to the ocean floor, where it remains out of sight. Environmental damage due to plastic debris is well documented. It includes:

* Mortality or sub-lethal effects when plastic is ingested by animals such as turtles, small-toothed whales and seabirds
* Entanglement of animals such as dolphins and large whales in nylon fishing gear (like nets) and other plastic debris
* Damage to critical ecosystems such as coral reefs and smothering of sediments
* Chemical contamination of marine organisms through ingestion of small plastic particles
* Potential changes in biodiversity due to the transport of invasive species on plastic fragments

Exposure of plastic to the ocean's physical, chemical and biological processes results in fragmentation and size reduction. Plastic on the seafloor will take far longer to fragment (due to lack of UV penetration and the cold water temperatures at these depths) than plastic on beaches or in surface waters near coastal areas. Plastic is extremely persistent in the marine environment.

Media reports and the activities of non-governmental organizations (NGOs) have improved awareness of the worldwide problem of plastic debris accumulating in the ocean, often focusing on its environmental impacts. In addition, the fishing and tourism industries in many countries are economically affected by the presence of plastic debris, which can enter nets, foul propellers and litter beaches. A growing concern is the possible contamination of fish and other marine organisms that ingest plastic debris and the possible adverse impacts on ecosystems and human health.

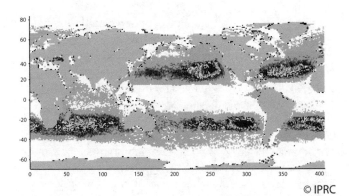

© IPRC

Gyres

Marine debris is subject to transport by ocean currents and tends to accumulate in a limited number of subtropical convergence zones or gyres. These gyres occur in the North and South Atlantic Ocean, the North and South Pacific, and the Indian Ocean.

Read more about plastic debris in the ocean in the UNEP Year Book 2011.

© NOAA Marine Debris Programme

Growing concern about microplastics

Plastic is now the most frequently reported material in encounters between debris and fish, sea birds, marine reptiles (e.g. turtles) and mammals (e.g. whales). As science progresses, more is being learned about the relationships between different types of mass-produced plastic and the organic contaminants they transport.

Concern is growing about the threat *microplastics* could present to marine life, including as a pathway for the transport of harmful chemicals through the food web. Ingestion of microplastics has been widely reported in a range of marine organisms including seabirds, fish, mussels, lugworms and zooplankton. Microplastics have also been identified as an emerging threat to much larger organisms, such as the endangered northern right whale, a surface-feeding baleen whale potentially exposed to microplastic ingestion as a result of its filter-feeding activity. The evidence is still insufficient, however, to quantify the nature and full extent of the effects of microplastics.

Microplastics

Microplastics are formed when plastic items fragment and disintegrate. The rate of fragmentation is highly dependent on the environmental setting, especially temperature and the amount of UV light available. Microplastics are also manufactured for use in plastic production, for other industrial purposes such as sand blasting, or for use in consumer (e.g. personal care) products. The term 'microplastics' is widely used to describe plastic particles with an upper size limit of 5 mm in diameter, which is the size range most readily ingested by many organisms. However, microplastics in products can be as small as 0.004 μm.

Plastic is increasingly found in the world's marine ecosystems. Every part of the ocean examined so far has revealed its presence. Microplastics were recently discovered in Arctic sea ice. Since sea ice is thinning, these small particles will likely be shed back into the water where they can be ingested by plankton, fish and other organisms.

Growth in plastics production 1950-2012

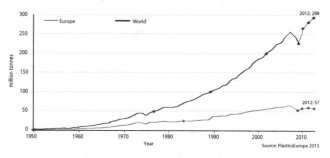

Increasing attention is being given to the use of microplastics in a wide range of consumer goods. 'Microbeads' are found in toothpaste, douche gels and facial cleansers, among other products, sometimes replacing natural ingredients (e.g. pumice or ground seeds). These microplastics tend not to be filtered out during wastewater treatment, but to be released directly to the ocean or other water bodies such as lakes and rivers. Microplastics are also found in effluent as tiny fibres after synthetic textiles are washed.

Diverse communities of microbes have been discovered colonizing and thriving on microplastics at multiple locations in the North Atlantic described as the 'plastisphere'. One concern about the plastisphere is that it can facilitate the transport of harmful microbes, including disease-causing pathogens and harmful algal species.

© NOAA Marine Debris Programme

Cooperation at international, regional and national levels

The disposal of plastic at sea is outlawed under Annex V of the International Maritime Organization (IMO) MARPOL Convention, which is designed to limit the impact of shipping and other maritime activities on the environment. Regional Seas bodies have introduced controls and monitoring guidance aimed at reducing inputs of plastic at a regional level. Many countries have begun to investigate potential control measures that could reduce these inputs cost-effectively. However, legislation alone is unlikely to be effective in bringing about significant reductions in the amount of plastic debris in the ocean. That will require changes in attitudes and behaviour by everyone.

NGOs, teachers, student groups, research institutes and others continue to organize activities to address the problem of plastic debris in the ocean. These range from providing participatory research and education for young people, to gathering innovative ideas from individuals and businesses; and from beach clean-ups in which local communities take part, to policy advocacy aimed at governmental bodies. Awareness raising is often one of the main objectives of these activities. For example, artwork comprising familiar plastic objects (e.g. shoes, toothbrushes, cigarette lighters) collected from the shoreline can convey a powerful message. On a different scale, the Plastiki, a 18-metre catamaran made of 12,500 reclaimed plastic bottles and other recycled PET plastic and waste products, sailed from San Francisco in the United States to Sydney, Australia, to bring attention to plastic pollution of the Atlantic Ocean.

The number of scientific studies concerned with plastic in marine ecosystems has rapidly increased and research is now expanding to freshwater systems. For example, microplastics have been found in Lake Garda in Italy and the Great Lakes in North America. Several international cooperative initiatives are under way to determine the physical and chemical effects of microplastics. One is a global assessment of the sources, fate and effects of microplastics in the marine environment by the Joint Group of Experts on the Scientific Aspects of Marine Environmental Protection (GESAMP).

In some countries, monitoring and central reporting of marine debris has taken place for some time. Determining the levels of microplastics from consumer products in water bodies is a more recent activity. Increasingly, the focus is widening towards the use of citizen science and mobile technology to collect data on the environment. The European Union (EU) Marine Strategy Framework Directive describes the status of the marine environment with the help of eleven indicators, one of which is the volume of marine litter. This indicator covers both larger particles visible to the human eye and microscopic particles. Exploratory investigations are under way to determine the levels of microplastics in four of Europe's major rivers.

Industry has been actively engaged in discussions about plastic debris in the ocean and important advances have been made in plastic recycling techniques. In 2011, the global plastics industry issued a declaration committing itself to contribute in various ways to solutions for marine litter. The 'beat the microbead' campaign aims to put pressure on companies to ban use of microplastics in products and inform customers via an app. As a result, a number of personal care and retail companies have announced they will stop producing or selling products containing microplastics.

In June 2012, the Global Partnership on Marine Litter (GPML) was established with the objective of protecting human health and the environment through the reduction and management of marine litter. The GPML works as an overall coordinating multi-stakeholder forum to increase awareness of the impacts of marine litter and to enhance knowledge and best practices.

© Aani Adriani and Graham Uden

The key to reducing inputs of plastic debris is at the source

Every effort should be made to prevent more plastic debris entering the ocean. However, production trends, use patterns and changing demographics are expected to result in ever greater amounts of plastic debris – including microplastics. Even if it were possible to keep more plastic from entering the environment, the amount already in the ocean will continue to break down into smaller fragments and to form microplastics for hundreds of years to come.

There is wide agreement that a safer and cleaner marine environment (including protection of marine animals and of human health) is a desirable goal, but feasible ways to remove the plastic and harmful chemicals already in the environment still appear to be very limited. Nevertheless, there are many opportunities to keep more plastic items from finding their way to the ocean.

The Plastic Disclosure Project encourages businesses and institutions to measure annual plastic use or waste aggregation in their operations. Awareness campaigns continue to be needed to discourage littering and convince people to reuse or ban plastic bags, among other actions. Introducing financial incentives for re-use or recycling (e.g. introducing levies on plastic packaging) and enforcing legislation to decrease the amount of plastic debris in the environment can lead to far greater recycling and waste prevention. Proposals are frequently made to turn plastic debris into a variety of products, or to use the plastic as fuel.

© Bill Macdonald

An important contribution is required from industry, together with universities and other research bodies, to find ways to reduce the impacts of plastic throughout its life cycle. This could include research on biodegradable resins, alternative ingredients, redesigned products, and next-generation additives that do not adversely impact the environment and human health. Apart from innovations in solid waste management, sewage treatment could be improved in order to trap smaller particles before effluent is discharged to surface water and sludge is deposited.

There is an immediate need to fill knowledge gaps and better understand the capacity of various types of plastic to sorb persistent, toxic and bioaccumulating chemicals (PBTs). Since plastic particles contaminated with these chemicals can potentially be ingested by marine organisms, the potential delivery of toxins through the food web via this mechanism needs to be further investigated and quantified if this can be shown to occur.

© Plastic Disclosure Project

For video links please go to http://vimeo.com/88804648

Further information about plastic debris in the ocean

Andrady, A.L. (2011). Microplastics in the marine environment. Marine Pollution Bulletin, 62, 1596-1605 www.sciencedirect.com/science/article/pii/S0025326X11003055

Bergmann, M. and Klages, M. (2012). Increase of litter at the Arctic deep-sea observatory HAUSGARTEN. Marine Pollution Bulletin, 64, 12 www.sciencedirect.com/science/article/pii/S0025326X12004687

Brown, J.A., et al. (2013). Microplastic Moves Pollutants and Additives to Worms, Reducing Functions Linked to Health and Biodiversity. Current Biology, 23, 23, 2388-2392 http://www.cell.com/current-biology/issue?pii=S0960-9822%2813%29X0023-5

Brown, M.A., et al. (2011). Accumulation of Microplastic on Shorelines Worldwide: Sources and Sinks. Environmental Science & Technology, 45, 21, 9175-9179 http://pubs.acs.org/doi/abs/10.1021/es201811s?journalCode=esthag

CBD/STAP-GEF (Secretariat of the Convention on Biological Diversity and the Scientific and Technical Advisory Panel-Global Environment Facility) (2012). Impacts of Marine Debris on Biodiversity: Current Status and Potential Solutions www.thegef.org/gef/sites/thegef.org/files/publication/cbd-ts-67-en.pdf

Codina-Garcia, M. (2013). Plastic debris in Mediterranean seabirds. Marine Pollution Bulletin, 77, 15, 220-226 http://www.sciencedirect.com/science/article/pii/S0025326X13006048

Cole, M., et al. (2011). Microplastics as contaminants in the marine environment: a review. Marine Pollution Bulletin, 62, 12, 2588-2589 www.ncbi.nlm.nih.gov/pubmed/22001295

Cole, M., et al. (2013). Microplastic Ingestion by Zooplankton. Environmental Science & Technology, 47, 12, 6646-6655. http://pubs.acs.org/doi/abs/10.1021/es400663f

Deltares (2014). First survey of microplastics in rivers http://www.deltares.nl/en/news/news-item/item/16968/first-survey-of-microplastics-in-rivers

Engler, R.E. (2012). The complex interaction between marine debris and toxic chemicals in the ocean. Environmental Science & Technology, 46, 22, 12302-12315 http://water.epa.gov/type/oceb/marinedebris/upload/The-Complex-Interaction-between-MD-and-Toxic-Chemicals-in-the-Ocean.pdf

Fossi, M.C., et al. (2012). Are baleen whales exposed to the threat of microplastics? A case study of the Mediterranean fin whale (Balaenoptera physalus). Marine Pollution Bulletin, 11, 2374-2379 www.sciencedirect.com/science/article/pii/S0025326X12004122

GESAMP (Joint Group of Experts on the Scientific Aspects of Marine Environmental Protection) Working Group 40 (2013). Sources, fate and effects of micro-plastics in the marine environment – a global assessment www.gesamp.org/work-programme/workgroups/working-group-40

Johnston, C. (2013). Personal Grooming Products May Be Harming Great Lakes Marine Life. Could removing dead skin cells from your face each night mean doom for perch and other Great Lakes species? Scientific American, 25 June. www.scientificamerican.com/article.cfm?id=microplastic-pollution-in-the-great-lakes

Kiesewetter, M.K., et al. (2010). Organocatalysis: Opportunities and Challenges for Polymer Synthesis. Macromolecules, 43, 5, 2093-2107 http://pubs.acs.org/doi/abs/10.1021/ma9025948

Lebreton, L.C.-M., et al. (2012). Numerical modeling of floating debris in the world's oceans. Marine Pollution Bulletin, 64, 653-661 www.sciencedirect.com/science/article/pii/S0025326X11005674

Lee, et al. (2013). Sorption capacity of plastic debris for hydrophobic organic chemicals. Science of the Total Environment www.sciencedirect.com/science/article/pii/S0048969713009376

Malmquist, D. (2013). Partnership aims to reduce pollution from "microplastics". Biodegradable "microbe-ads" meant to breakdown before entering waterways. News release, Virginia Institute of Marine Science www.wm.edu/news/stories/2013/partnership-aims-to-reduce-pollution-from-microplastics221.php

Martin, J.M. (2013). Marine debris removal: One year of effort by the Georgia Sea Turtle Center Marine Debris Initiative. Marine Pollution Bulletin, 15, 74, 1, 165-169 http://www.sciencedirect.com/science/article/pii/S0025326X13003780

NOAA (United States National Oceanic and Atmospheric Administration) (2013). Marine Debris Program http://marinedebris.noaa.gov/

Pham, C.K., et al. (2014). Marine Litter Distribution and Density in European Seas, from the Shelves to Deep Basins. PLOS ONE, 30 April http://www.plosone.org/article/info%3Adoi%2F10.1371%2Fjournal.pone.0095839

Rochman, C.M., et al. (2013), Long-Term Field Measurement of Sorption of Organic Contaminants to Five Types of Plastic Pellets: Implications for Plastic Marine Debris. Environmental Science & Technology, 47, 3, 1646-1654 http://pubs.acs.org/doi/abs/10.1021/es303700s

Thompson, R.C. (2013). Written evidence on microplastics submitted to the Science and Technology Committee, Parliament of the United Kingdom www.publications.parliament.uk/pa/cm201314/cmselect/cmsctech/272/272we13.htm

UNEP (2011). UNEP Year Book 2011: Emerging Issues in our Global Environment http://www.unep.org/yearbook/2011

UNEP (2014). 'Globally-emitted Contaminants Affecting SIDS' in Emerging issues for Small Island Developing States. Results of the UNEP Foresight Process http://www.unep.org/pdf/Emerging_issues_for_small_island_developing_states.pdf

Watters, D.L., et al. (2010). Assessing marine debris in deep seafloor habitats off California. Marine Pollution Bulletin, 60, 131–138. http://www.lovelab.id.ucsb.edu/Watters%20et%20al.%202010.pdf

Woods Hole Oceanographic Institution (2013). Scientists Discover Thriving Colonies of Microbe in Ocean 'Plastisphere. News release www.whoi.edu/page.do?pid=7545&tid=3622&cid=171469

Wright, S.L., et al. (2013). Microplastic ingestion decreases energy reserves in marine worms. Current Biology, 23, 23, 1031-1033 http://www.cell.com/current-biology/abstract/S0960-9822(13)01343-2

Wright, S.L., et al. (2013). The physical impacts of microplastics on marine organisms: a review. Environmental Pollution, 178, 483-92 www.ncbi.nlm.nih.gov/pubmed/23545014

Zettler, E.R., et al. (2013). Life in the "Plastisphere": Microbial Communities on Plastic Marine Debris. Environmental Science & Technology, 47, 13, 7137-7146 http://pubs.acs.org/doi/abs/10.1021/es401288x

UNEP Year Book 2014 emerging issues update

Securing Soil Carbon Benefits

Managing soils for multiple economic, societal and environmental benefits

Soil is essential for agricultural production. The carbon in soil plays a vital role in regulating the world's climate, water supplies and biodiversity – and therefore in providing numerous ecosystem services. However, soil carbon is highly vulnerable to human activities.

Around 60% of the carbon in the world's soils and vegetation has been lost since the 19th century. The current rate of change in soil organic carbon is mainly attributable to worldwide intensification of land use and conversion of uncultivated land for food, feed, fibre and fuel production. As a result of soil carbon losses in the last 25 years or so, one-quarter of the global land area has declined in agricultural productivity and the ability to provide ecosystem services.

Over double the amount of carbon held in the atmosphere is stored in the top metre of the world's soils. Accelerated decomposition due to land use change (e.g. deforestation) and unsustainable land management practices causes soils to release carbon dioxide (CO_2) and other greenhouse gases.

Soil erosion associated with conventional agricultural practices can occur at rates up to 100 times greater than the rate at which natural soil formation takes place. Peatland drainage worldwide is causing carbon-rich peat to disappear at a rate 20 times greater than the rate at which

it accumulated. If present trends continue, there will be rapid losses of soil carbon to the atmosphere in the future, exacerbating climate change and increasing the extent of global soil degradation. These losses will put food, feed, fibre and fuel crop production at risk, while a wide range of vital ecosystem services will continue to be diminished.

Because of its central role in so many ecosystem services, soil carbon also offers hope for solutions to global challenges. Soil is an integrating component of the Earth's surface that links the above-ground and below-ground environments, collectively termed the *Earth's Critical Zone*. Thus soil is a vital control point where managed human interventions to increase soil carbon stocks can provide multiple, wide-ranging benefits for food and water security, biomass production and greenhouse gas mitigation.

Read more about soil carbon benefits in the UNEP Year Book 2012.

The Earth's Critical Zone

The Critical Zone, linking the above-ground and below-ground environments, is referred to as 'critical' because this thin surface layer provides most life-sustaining resources. Soil is an essential link in the chain of impact that propagates the effects of above-ground environmental change, such as climate and land use transitions, throughout the Critical Zone.

Global variation in soil organic carbon (SOC) density, 0-1 m depth

SOC Density
t C/ha

5-40
40 - 60
60 - 85
85 - 150
>150

Source: FAO/IIASA/ISRIC/ISSCAS/JRC, 2012

© Elke Noellemeyer

Improved soil management: crucial for climate change and food production

Scientific understanding of the benefits of soil carbon has increased in recent years – stimulated by the potential contribution of soils to climate change mitigation and the need for more sustainable agricultural development, including better management of soils. Due to the complexity of soil systems, knowledge about soil carbon is fragmented across many science disciplines and economic sectors. Recently, scientists undertook a *Rapid Assessment Process* integrating scientific evidence of the multiple benefits of soil carbon and exploring how new policy and management practices can help deliver these benefits more rapidly and more widely around the world.

© Hans Joosten

Rapid assessment process on soil organic carbon

Following production of the UNEP Year Book 2012 chapter on soil carbon, the Scientific Committee on Problems of the Environment (SCOPE) initiated a Rapid Assessment Process that amassed scientific evidence from more than 80 experts worldwide, resulting in the preparation of 27 chapters over an 18-month period on the multiple benefits of soil carbon and their implementation in policy and practice. This work culminated in a five-day workshop in 2013 that prepared four cross-cutting chapters of recommendations for policy in soil and land management practice and a SCOPE publication.

Studies continue to show that soil carbon stocks throughout the world are strongly affected by land use and land management, as well as by environmental conditions. Soil organic carbon is the largest constituent of soil organic matter, which also contains nutrients essential for plant growth such as nitrogen, phosphorus, sulphur and micronutrients. The amount and dynamics of soil organic matter are major determinants of the quantity and quality of ecosystem services. Improving land use and management to enhance carbon storage is integral to global efforts to feed a growing population and address climate change (e.g. through carbon sequestration).

Intensive commercial agriculture tends to reduce carbon stocks, while sustainable agriculture has the potential to increase them. Significant changes in soil organic carbon stocks can occur within several decades. The results of sustainable soil management could be noticeable over similar periods.

A wide range of ecosystem services require healthy soils and soil biodiversity. Yet the pressure on soil for various land uses remains enormous, undermining the very basis of agricultural production. It is clear that maintaining minimum levels of soil organic carbon is essential to overall soil health, apart from the contribution this resource makes to climate change mitigation. Increasing soil organic carbon above minimum levels is a form of pro-active management to achieve additional benefits. While governments consider goals and targets for food security, soil scientists are carrying out assessments and looking for practical ways to determine, measure and maintain healthy levels of soil organic carbon.

Maintaining and enhancing soil carbon benefits

In agriculture, the purpose of many ongoing research and development efforts is to improve land management. For example, *conservation agriculture* initiatives in developing countries are aimed at increasing soil organic carbon and reducing its losses while improving farmers' incomes and alleviating poverty. The effectiveness of measures to increase carbon inputs to agricultural soils and reduce carbon losses depends on local conditions, including soil types and climate.

Conservation agriculture

The purpose of conservation agriculture is to achieve sustainable and profitable agriculture, and improved livelihoods for farmers, through the application of three principles: minimal soil disturbance, permanent soil cover, and crop rotations. Conservation agriculture was reportedly practised on 117 million hectares worldwide in 2010.

The rate of global forest clearance has accelerated due to population growth and demand for food, feed, fibre, fuel – and living space. Over 5 million hectares of forest has been cleared annually in recent years. Soil carbon is lost rapidly as a result of forest clearance. Preventing forest loss and degradation (e.g. under the UN-REDD programme) has multiple benefits in addition to protecting and enhancing carbon stocks. These benefits include water regulation and biodiversity conservation.

The Food and Agriculture Organization (FAO) Global Forest Resources Assessments are produced every five years to provide an update on the state of the world's forests and how they are changing. The recently launched Global Forest Watch is an online forest monitoring and alert system that gives near real-time information about changes in forests. Its goal is to empower people everywhere to better manage forests – which can have significant impacts on soil carbon stocks. Created by UNEP, the World Resources Institute and more than 40 partners, it uses satellite technology, open data and crowd sourcing to support monitoring of global forest status.

Conserving and restoring *peatlands* and improving their management can greatly benefit soil carbon conservation and contribute to avoiding greenhouse gas emissions. The first international conference on the use of emergent wetland plants, 'Reed as a Renewable Resource', took place in 2013. This is one of a number of research and other activities carried out in recent years to encourage wetlands protection, restoration and utilization to provide multiple ecosystem services, including carbon sequestration and storage.

Peatland protection

Peatlands cover about 3% of the Earth's land area, but contain some 30% of total soil carbon. While the majority of peatlands are still in a natural state, many have been drained and degraded. Unlike carbon emissions associated with forest clearance – which are largely instantaneous – those from drained peatlands continue as long as the peatland remains drained. Drained peatlands emit almost 6% of anthropogenic CO_2 emissions. Peatland conservation, restoration and improved management is therefore critical for climate change mitigation.

© Concern Worldwide

For video links please go to http://www.youtube.com/watch?v=YXbIRCKWTfU

Seeking synergies with other policy objectives

Appropriate soil management helps to meet some of the greatest challenges the world faces, including food and energy security, water availability and quality, climate change adaptation and mitigation, biodiversity conservation, and the health and well-being of billions of people.

Opportunities exist at every level (global, regional, national, local) to enhance soil carbon and avoid losses of this precious resource. In some countries these may include, for example, restricting the conversion of woodland and grassland to arable crops. A major challenge is to improve understanding of the urgency of using these opportunities. This is essential if adequate resources are to be made available for planning, developing and implementing the necessary policies, actions and incentive mechanisms.

Policy-makers are increasingly called upon to make decisions that involve conflicting demands for food, feed, fibre, fuel and forest crops, as well as climate regulation, water, biodiversity conservation, living space and other needs. It may be necessary to protect soils that provide important soil carbon storage and other benefits, such as peatlands, despite pressures to convert them to uses that could be more economically profitable in the short term.

The Global Soil Partnership, an international initiative launched in 2011 and operated by the FAO, is aimed at improving global governance of soil resources by advocating (and coordinating) initiatives to ensure that knowledge and recognition of soils are appropriately represented in global change dialogues and decision-making processes. Its work is carried out under five *pillars of action*.

Recommendations made during Global Soil Week 2013 (convened within the framework of the Global Soil Partnership) included strengthening the policy-science interface and increasing soil carbon synergies in policy-making process through the Intergovernmental Platform on Biodiversity and Ecosystem Services (IPBES), the United Nations Convention to Combat Desertification (UNCCD) and

its Committee on Science and Technology, and renewed food security policy activities.

The Global Soil Partnership's five pillars of action

- Promote sustainable management of soil resources for soil protection, conservation and sustainable productivity
- Encourage investment, technical cooperation, policy, education, awareness and extension in soil
- Promote targeted soil research and development focusing on identified gaps and priorities and synergies with related productive, environmental and social development actions
- Enhance the quantity and quality of soil data and information through data collection and generation, analysis, validation, reporting, monitoring, and integration with other disciplines
- Harmonize methods, measurements and indicators for the sustainable management and protection of soil resources

© UNCCD

Further information about soil carbon benefits

Banwart, S., et al. (2014). Benefits of soil carbon: Report on the outcomes of an international Scientific Committee on Problems of the Environment (SCOPE) Rapid Assessment Workshop. Biofuels and Carbon Management. Special issue, April 2014

Banwart, S.A., Noellemeyer, E., Milne, E. (2014). Soil Carbon: Science, management and policy for multiple benefits. SCOPE Series Vol. 71. CABI, Wallingford (in press)

Corsi, S., et al. (2012). Soil Organic Carbon Accumulation and Greenhouse Gas Emission Reductions from Conservation Agriculture: A literature review. Integrated Crop Management, Vol. 16. FAO, Rome http://www.fao.org/fileadmin/user_upload/agp/icm16.pdf

De Sanctis, P.P., et al. (2012). Long-term no tillage increased soil organic carbon content of rain-fed cereal systems in a Mediterranean area. European Journal of Agronomy 40, 18-27 http://www.sciencedirect.com/science/article/pii/S1161030112000238

Eagle, A.J., et al. (2012). Greenhouse Gas Mitigation Potential of Agricultural Land Management in the United States: A synthesis of the literature (3rd ed.). Nicholas Institute for Environmental Policy Solutions, USA. http://nicholasinstitute.duke.edu/sites/default/files/publications/ni_r_10-04_3rd_edition.pdf

Gattinger, A., et al. (2012). Enhanced top soil carbon stocks under organic farming. Proceedings of the National Academy of Sciences of the United States, 109, 44, 18226-18231 http://www.pnas.org/content/109/44/18226.abstract

Govers, G., et al. (2013). Managing Soil Organic Carbon for Global Benefits: A STAP Technical Report. Global Environment Facility, Washington, D.C. http://www.thegef.org/gef/pubs/managing-soil-organic-carbon-global-benefits

Hiederer, R. and Köchy, M. (2012). Global soil organic carbon estimates and the harmonized world soil database. European Commission, Joint Research Centre-Institute for Environment and Sustainability (JRC-IES, Luxembourg. http://eusoils.jrc.ec.europa.eu/esdb_archive/eusoils_docs/other/EUR25225.pdf

Ladd, B., et al. (2013). Estimates of soil carbon concentration in tropical and temperate forest and woodland from available GIS data on three continents. Global Ecology and Biogeography, 22, 461-469. http://onlinelibrary.wiley.com/doi/10.1111/j.1466-8238.2012.00799.x/abstract

Mäkipää, R., et al. (2012). Soil carbon monitoring using surveys and modeling. General description and application in the United Republic of Tanzania. Forestry Paper 168. FAO, Rome http://www.fao.org/fileadmin/user_upload/agp/icm16.pdf

Ogle, S.M., et al. (2012). No-till management impacts on crop productivity, carbon input and soil carbon sequestration. Agriculture, Ecosystems & Environment, 149, 37-49. http://www.sciencedirect.com/science/article/pii/S0167880911004361

Qin, Z., et al. (2013). Soil organic carbon sequestration potential of cropland in China. Global Biogeochemical Cycles, 27, 3, 711-722. http://onlinelibrary.wiley.com/doi/10.1002/gbc.20068/full

Royal Society of Chemistry (2012). Securing Soils for Sustainable Agriculture: A science-led strategy. London. http://www.rsc.org/images/081203%20OSCAR%20web_tcm18-222767.pdf

Stockmann, U., et al. (2013). The knowns, known unknowns and unknowns of sequestration of soil organic carbon. Agriculture, Ecosystems & Environment, 164, 80-99. http://www.sciencedirect.com/science/article/pii/S0167880912003635

UNEP (United Nations Environment Programme) (2012). "The benefits of soil carbon: Managing soils for multiple economic, societal and environmental benefits." In: UNEP Year Book 2012: Emerging Issues in Our Global Environment. http://www.unep.org/yearbook/2012/pdfs/UYB_2012_CH_2.pdf

UNEP Year Book 2014 emerging issues update

Rapid Change in the Arctic

A view from the top

The UNEP Year Book 2013 reported unprecedented loss of summer sea ice in 2012 as a result of warming in the Arctic. At 3.4 million km^2, the minimum sea ice extent that year was 18% below the previous record minimum in 2007. Besides loss of summer sea ice, Arctic warming threatens the region's biodiversity. Arctic warming also could also have far-reaching consequences for global ocean circulation and weather patterns, migratory species that visit the Arctic, and potential greenhouse gas emissions from the thawing of *permafrost*. Permafrost thawing and the loss of snow and ice on land both contribute to global sea level rise.

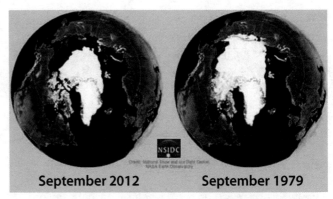

September 2012   September 1979

© NSIDC, NASA Earth Observatory

Permafrost: long-frozen ground

Permafrost is a layer of frozen soil at some depth below the surface, where the temperature has continuously been below 0°C for at least several years. It has been retreating northwards in many places in the Arctic as the climate warms. Permafrost soils often contain large volumes of organic carbon. As these soils thaw, irreversible releases of some of the carbon in the form of greenhouse gases (CO_2 and methane) will occur, thereby reinforcing climate change.

Rapid changes in the Arctic require urgent responses within the region and from the wider world. Since climate change dominates the current transformation of the Arctic environment, reducing global greenhouse gas emissions is the most important action that needs to be taken.

Read more about rapid change in the Arctic in the UNEP Year Book 2013.

Global climate change is emerging as the most important stressor for Arctic biodiversity. Rapidly changing ice conditions due to Arctic warming affect life on land and in the sea. In particular, iconic animals that live on the ice such as polar bears, walruses and seals are at risk. The Arctic Ocean is especially prone to ocean acidification, as colder waters can hold more carbon dioxide (CO_2) than warmer ones.

Retreating sea ice offers new opportunities for resource exploitation, trade, and economic development. Use of northern shipping routes is already increasing. Mining and oil, gas and mineral exploitation are expanding, as are commercial fisheries. Such opportunities also present challenges for the region, including environmental risks and social concerns regarding its local and indigenous inhabitants.

> ❝ The Arctic is changing twice as fast in terms of warming as the rest of the world. What happens to migratory species in the Arctic will affect what happens in the overwintering grounds of those species, and what happens to the melting glaciers and permafrost thaw will affect sea level rise in the rest of the world. ❞
>
> – Terry Callaghan,
> Royal Swedish Academy of Sciences

Arctic update: science and shipping

In general, rapid warming in the Arctic is continuing. This affects marine and land ecosystems within the region, as well as people and livelihoods. Cooler temperatures across the central Arctic Ocean, Greenland and North Canada in the summer of 2013 helped to moderate the record loss of sea ice and melting of the Greenland ice sheet experienced the previous year. Nevertheless, the extent of summer sea ice was the sixth lowest since observations began in 1979.

New assessments are highlighting the impact of climate change on Arctic marine and terrestrial environments. A comprehensive report on ocean acidification in the region, released by the Arctic Council, confirms that among the world's oceans the Arctic Ocean is one of the most sensitive to ocean acidification, and that Arctic marine ecosystems are highly likely to undergo significant changes as a result.

Another Arctic Council report, the 'Arctic Biodiversity Assessment', confirms that climate change is the most important stressor for Arctic biodiversity and will exacerbate all other threats. Increased human activities such as oil exploration and shipping will place additional stress on the region's biodiversity.

Scientific understanding of *black carbon* as a global climate warming agent is advancing rapidly. There is also better understanding of its importance in Arctic warming. When black carbon is deposited on snow and ice, the soot-covered surface absorbs more sunlight, leading to surface warming. Owing to the large amount of snow and ice in the Arctic, this region is likely to be especially sensitive to black carbon. Black carbon emitted within the Arctic has an almost five times greater warming effect than black carbon from outside the region. There are currently few sources of black carbon within the Arctic, but such sources are expected to grow with increased oil and gas production, shipping and other human activities.

Investments and activities for the purpose of extracting oil and gas in the Arctic are growing. For example, interest in

Black carbon: a short-lived climate pollutant

Formed by incomplete combustion of fossil fuels, biofuels and biomass, black carbon is emitted directly to the atmosphere in the form of fine particles. It is a major component of soot (a complex dark mixture) and it contributes to global warming by absorbing heat in the atmosphere and by reducing the ability to reflect sunlight when deposited on snow and ice. Unlike CO_2, which has a long atmospheric lifetime, black carbon remains in the atmosphere only several days to weeks.

exploiting the Barents Sea region north of Norway and Russia was recently stimulated by the announcement of large, previously undiscovered reserves. In some other parts of the Arctic, however, drilling has been postponed or delayed due to safety concerns.

Marine shipping in the Arctic is increasing. As of September 2013, the Northern Sea Route Administration had issued 495 permits to navigate and operate along this route – a nearly four-fold increase compared to 2012. However, most of the 2013 permits were for the western parts of Russian waters rather than for transit routes.

© Björn Alfthan/GRID-Arendal

Adapting to rapid change

In 2013 the Arctic states, under the auspices of the Arctic Council, signed a new, legally binding Agreement on Cooperation on Marine Oil Pollution Preparedness and Response in the Arctic. It provides a framework for co-operation in the event of an emergency, in order to improve procedures for combating oil spills in the Arctic. This is an important first step towards ensuring the safety of the Arctic environment and its inhabitants. It follows from the Arctic Search and Rescue Agreement, signed in 2011.

The Arctic Council working groups have made an essential contribution to understanding rapid change in the Arctic, in some cases spurring global action. Arctic scientific work as part of the Global Mercury Assessment has been widely recognized for its contribution to the new Minamata Convention on Mercury, which limits harmful mercury emissions. The Task Force on Short-Lived Climate Forcers has been active in developing the scientific agenda and recommendations for reducing black carbon and methane emissions in Arctic states. Moreover, Arctic states have been identifying areas of heightened ecological and cultural significance in light of the changing climate and multiple and growing marine uses – suggesting ways to protect these areas from the impacts of Arctic marine shipping.

The International Maritime Organization (IMO) is currently developing a draft International code of safety for ships operating in polar waters (the Polar Code), which would cover the full range of design, construction, equipment, operational training, search and rescue and environmental protection matters relevant to ships operating in inhospitable waters surrounding the two poles.

Russia has announced the creation of a national park, Beringia, in the remote Far Eastern Region of Chukotka. This new park will touch the United States maritime border in the Bering Strait. The creation of a new national park on the Russian side paves the way for a joint US-Russian nature reserve spanning the Strait.

© Lawrence Hislop/GRID-Arendal

Many Indigenous organizations are actively involved in monitoring rapid changes in the environment and are seeking ways to adapt to these changes. All the Permanent Participants of the Arctic Council, as well as many other indigenous organisations, run projects, ranging from strengthening indigenous participation in decision-making processes to documenting and enhancing use of traditional knowledge.

© Arctic Council

For video links please go to http://www.arctic-council.org/index.php/en/events/meetings-overview/kiruna-ministerial-2013

Combatting climate change and building resilience

To respond to the rapid change in the Arctic, building *resilience* and adapting to inevitable climate change is of great importance. Resilience is the long-term capacity to deal with change and continue to develop and adapt within critical thresholds.

Ecosystem and social resilience

Ecosystem resilience is a measure of how much disturbance an ecosystem can handle (e.g. in the form of storms, fire or pollutants) without shifting into a qualitatively different state. It is the capacity of a system to both withstand shocks and surprises and to rebuild itself if damaged. Social resilience is the ability of human communities to withstand and recover from stresses such as environmental change or social, economic or political upheaval. Resilience in societies and their life-supporting ecosystems is crucial in order to maintain options for future human development.

© Phillip Burgess/International Centre for Reindeer Husbandry

In view of the potential for major environmental damage, careful consideration needs to be given to a precautionary approach to economic development. A precautionary approach requires measures such as development moratoriums until full assessments have established risks to the environment and human systems – and until adequate management frameworks are in place. Because of the rapid pace of change in the fragile Arctic region, it is essential to develop strengthened systems for monitoring and for provision of early warnings.

The leading scientific research being carried out in the Arctic, and successful inter-governmental cooperation on protecting the region's environment, provide examples for the rest of the world.

© Lawrence Hislop/GRID-Arendal

Further information about the Arctic

AMAP (Arctic Monitoring and Assessment Programme) (2013). AMAP Assessment 2013: Arctic Ocean Acidification http://www.amap.no/documents/doc/amap-assessment-2013-arctic-ocean-acidification/881

AMAP/CAFF (Conservation of Arctic Flora and Fauna)/ SDWG (Sustainable Development Working Group) (2013). Identification of Arctic marine areas of heightened ecological and cultural significance: Arctic Marine Shipping Assessment (AMSA) IIc http://www.amap.no/documents/doc/Identification-of-Arctic-marine-areas-of-heightened-ecological-and-cultural-significance-Arctic-Marine-Shipping-Assessment-AMSA-IIc/869

Arctic Centre, University of Lapland (2013). Arctic Indigenous Peoples http://www.arcticcentre.org/InEnglish/SCIENCE-COMMUNICATIONS/Arctic-region/Arctic-Indigenous-Peoples

Arctic Parliamentarians, Arctic governance in an evolving Arctic region http://www.arcticparl.org/files/arctic-governance-in-an-evolving-arctic-region.pdf

CAFF (2013). Arctic Biodiversity Assessment: Status and Trends in Arctic Biodiversity http://www.arcticbiodiversity.is/

Jeffries, M.O., Richter-Menge, J.A. and Overland, J.E. (eds.) (2013). Arctic Report Card: Update for 2013. Tracking recent environmental changes.

Sand, M., Berntsen, T.K., Seland, Ø. and Kristjánsson, J.E. (2013). Arctic surface temperature change to emissions of black carbon within Arctic or mid-latitudes. Journal of Geophysical Research, 118, 14, 7788-7798.

Screen, J.A., Simmonds, I. and Keay, K. (2011). Dramatic interannual changes of perennial Arctic sea ice linked to abnormal summer storm activity. Journal of Geophysical Research, 116, D15,

Sharma, S., Ogren, J.A., Jefferson, A., Eleftheriadis, K., Chan, E., Quinn, P.K. and Burkhart, J.K. (2013). Black Carbon in the Arctic. In: Arctic Report Card: Update for 2013.

Stohl, A., Klimont, Z., Eckhardt, S., Kupiainen, K., Shevchenko, V.P., Kopeikin, V.M. and Novigatsky, A.N. (2013). Black carbon in the Arctic: the under-estimated role of gas flaring and residential combustion engines. Atmospheric Chemistry and Physics, 13, 8833-8855.

UNEP (2013). The View from the Top: Searching for responses to a rapidly changing Arctic. In: UNEP Yearbook 2013: Emerging Issues of our Environment. UNEP Division of Early Warning and Assessment, Nairobi, Kenya.

World Economic Forum (2014). Demystifying the Arctic. Authored by the Members of the World Economic Forum Global Agenda Council on the Arctic. Davos-Klosters, Switzerland 22-25 January 2014

Acknowledgements

Excess nitrogen in the environment

Science writer

John Smith, **Austin, United States**

Reviewers

Anjan Datta, **UNEP, Nairobi, Kenya**
Jan Willem Erisman, **Louis Bolk Institute, Driebergen,**
The Netherlands

The emergence of infectious diseases

Science writer

Penny Park, **Science Media Centre of Canada, Toronto, Canada**

Reviewers

Kerry Bowman, **University of Toronto Joint Centre for Bioethics,**
Toronto, Canada
Richard Ostfeld, **Cary Institute of Ecosystem Studies, Millbrook,**
United States
Carolyn Stephens, **Universidad Nacional de Tucumán, Tucumán,**
Argentina

Fish and shellfish farming

Science writer

Christian Neumann, **GRID-Arendal, Arendal, Norway**

Reviewers

Lex Bouwman, **Netherlands Environmental Assessment Agency,**
The Hague , The Netherlands
Food and Agriculture Organization of the UN (FAO), **Aquaculture**
Branch, Rome, Italy
Patricia Glibert, **University of Maryland Center for Environmental**
Science, Cambridge, United States
Esther Luiten, **Aquaculture Stewardship Council, Utrecht, The**
Netherlands
Michael Phillips, **WorldFish, Penang, Malaysia**
Pinya Sarasas, **UNEP, Nairobi, Kenya**
Greg Sherley, **UNEP, Apia, Samoa**
Posa Skelton, **Secretariat of the Pacific Regional Environment**
Programme (SPREP), Apia, Samoa
WWF, **Gland, Switzerland**

Illegal trade in wildlife

Science writer

Penny Park, **Science Media Centre of Canada, Toronto, Canada**

Reviewers

Ludgarde Coppens, **UNEP, Nairobi, Kenya**
Bianca Notarbartolo di Sciara, **UNEP, Nairobi, Kenya**
Lisa Rolls Hagelberg, **UNEP, Nairobi, Kenya**
John Scanlon, **Convention on International Trade in**
Endangered Species of Wild Fauna and Flora (CITES), Geneva,
Switzerland

Realizing the potential of citizen science

Science writer

Penny Park, **Science Media Centre of Canada, Toronto, Canada**

Reviewers

Susanne Bech, **UN-Habitat, Nairobi, Kenya**
Rick Bonney, **Cornell Laboratory of Ornithology, New York,**
United States
Denis Couvet, **National Museum of Natural History**
(Department 'Ecology and Management of Biodiversity'), École
Polytechnique, Palaiseau, Paris, France
Muki Haklay, **University College London, London,**
United Kingdom
Tero Mustonen, **Snowchange Cooperative, North Karelia,**
Finland

Methane from hydrates

Science writer

John Smith, **Austin, United States**

Reviewers

Yannick Beaudoin, **GRID-Arendal, Arendal, Norway**
Robert Corell, **Global Environment and Technology Foundation**
and its Center for Energy and Climate Solution, Washington, DC,
United States
Carolyn Ruppel, **US Geological Survey's Gas Hydrates Project,**
Woods Hole, United States
Koji Yamamoto, **Japan Oil, Gas and Metals National Corporation**
(JOGMEC), Tokyo, Japan

Air pollution: world's worst environmental health risk

Science writer

John Smith, Austin, United States

Reviewers

Nils-Axel Braathen, Organisation for Economic Co-operation and Development (OECD), Paris, France
Volodymyr Demkine, UNEP, Nairobi, Kenya
Wei Huang, Peking University School of Public Health, Beijing, China
Rob de Jong, UNEP, Nairobi, Kenya
Nino Künzli, Swiss Tropical and Public Health Institute, Basel, Switzerland
Martina Otto, Secretariat of the Climate and Clean Air Coalition to Reduce Short-Lived Climate Pollutants (CCAC), Paris, France
Janak Pathak, UNEP, Nairobi, Kenya

Plastic debris in the ocean

Science writer

John Smith, Austin, United States

Reviewers

Peter Kershaw, Centre for Environment, Fisheries and Aquaculture Science, Lowestoft, United Kingdom
Liana McManus, Global Environment Facility Transboundary Waters Assessment Programme (GEF TWAP), Pembroke Pines, United States
Heidi Savelli, UNEP, Nairobi, Kenya

Securing soil carbon benefits

Science writer

John Smith, Austin, United States

Reviewers

Steven Banwart, Kroto Research Institute, University of Sheffield, United Kingdom
Gemma Shepherd, UNEP, Nairobi, Kenya
Ronald Vargas, FAO, Rome, Italy

Rapid change in the Arctic

Science writers

Björn Alfthan, GRID-Arendal, Arendal, Norway
Lawrence Hislop, GRID-Arendal, Arendal, Norway

Reviewers

Robert Corell, Global Environment and Technology Foundation and its Center for Energy and Climate Solutions, Washington, DC, United States
Markku Heikkilä, Science Communications, Arctic Center, Oulu, Finland
Svein Mathiesen, UArctic EALÁT Institute, Kautokeino, Norway
Peter Prokosch, GRID-Arendal, Arendal, Norway
Jon Samseth, SINTEF Materials and Chemistry, Trondheim, Norway
Adam Stepien, University of Lapland, Rovaniemi, Finland

UNEP Year Book 2014 production team

Project team

Tessa Goverse (editor-in-chief), Ali Malik, Nyokabi Mwangi, Trang Nguyen and Franklin Odhiambo, UNEP, Nairobi, Kenya; Susan Greenwood Etienne, Scientific Committee on Problems of the Environment (SCOPE), Paris, France; Márton Bálint, Budapest, Hungary

Copy editor

John Smith, Austin, United States

Graphics, design and layout

Josephat Kariuki, David Koch, Ali Malik, Chris Mungai and Audrey Ringler, UNEP, Nairobi, Kenya; Jinita Shah and Martin Michuki, UNON, Nairobi, Kenya; Márton Bálint, Budapest, Hungary; Rob Barnes and Judith Maréchal, GRID-Arendal, Arendal, Norway

Credits

Front cover image top: © Shyamalamuralinath/Shutterstock
Front cover image middle: © HPH Image Library/Shutterstock
Front cover image bottom: © Galyna Andrushko/Shutterstock
Back cover top left image: © Sayanjo65/Shutterstock
Back cover top right image: © Vladislav Gajic/Shutterstock
Back cover bottom left image: © Sergey Nivens/Shutterstock
Back cover bottom right image: © Tyler Olson/Shutterstock

Chapter image nitrogen: © Anton Foltin/Shutterstock
Chapter image infectious diseases: © motorolka/Shutterstock
Chapter image fish farming: © Gerard Koudenburg/Shutterstock
Chapter image illegal wildlife trade: © WWF
Chapter image methane hydrates: © USGS
Chapter image citizen science: © Gill Conquest/ExCiTeS
Chapter image air pollution: © ssuaphotos/Shutterstock
Chapter image plastic debris: © British Antarctic Survey
Chapter image soil carbon: © Hans Joosten
Chapter image Arctic: © Lawrence Hislop/GRID-Arendal

Digital
UNEP Year Book 2014
for iPad and Android

To view **UNEP Year Book 2014** digital edition
for iPad go to **iTunes App Store**
or for Android go to **Google Play**
and search for **'UNON PSS App'**,
install and enjoy...

UNON PUBLISHING SERVICES SECTION, NAIROBI, ISO 14001:2004-CERTIFIED UNON PUBLISHING SERVICES SECTION, NAIROBI UNON PUBLISHING SERVICES SECTION, NAIROBI, ISO 14001:2004-CERTIFIED UNON PUBLISHING SERVICES SECTION, NAIROBI UNON PUBLISHING SERVICES SECTION, NAIROBI, ISO 14001:2004-

**UNITED NATIONS
OFFICE AT NAIROBI**
The UN Headquarters in Africa

App created by UNON
Publishing Services Section
http://dcs.unon.org